POKER
WIT AND
WISDOM

Fiona Jerome
and Seth Dickson

A Think Book

THE WIT AND WISDOM SERIES

Poker Wit and Wisdom
By Fiona Jerome and Seth Dickson
From nineteenth-century Mississippi river boats to Cockney gambling dens and
.com casinos, *Poker Wit and Wisdom* takes a lingering look at the addictive
world of poker, dealing out all the oddities, quirks and stories along the way.
ISBN 1-84525-004-4

Wine Wit and Wisdom
By Maggie Rosen, Fiona Jerome and PJ Harris
A lingering look at the wonderful world of wine, *Wine Wit and Wisdom* blends
the banquets of Bacchus with the grapes of wrath, and the fruitiest flavours
with the correct way to judge a bouquet.
ISBN 1-84525-003-6

Series Editor
Malcolm Tait

The guy who invented poker was bright, but the guy who invented the chip was a genius.

Big Julie, Chicago Mobster

THINK
BOOKS

A Think Book

First published in Great Britain in 2005 by
Think Publishing
The Pall Mall Deposit
124-128 Barlby Road, London W10 6BL
www.think-books.com

Written by Fiona Jerome and Seth Dickson
Wit and Wisdom team: James Collins, Rica Dearman, Rhiannon Guy, Emma
Jones, Matt Packer, Sonja Patel, Mark Searle, Lou Millward and Malcolm Tait

ISBN 1-84525-004-4

Printed & bound in Great Britain by William Clowes Ltd, Beccles, Suffolk.

Cover image: Thom Lang/CORBIS

I believe in poker the way I believe in the American Dream.
Poker is good for you. It enriches the soul, sharpens the intellect,
heals the spirit, and – when played well, nourishes the wallet.

Lou Krieger

THANKS AND LUCKY FLOPS

Mike and Penny Dash for ideas, brain picking and access to their eclectic library

Andrew Littlefield for buying us our first Texas hold 'em set one Christmas

John Innes for suggesting the idea of a book in the first place

Bill and Janet Kingdon for saving clippings

Martin Skidmore for selflessly offering up his friends as
guinea pigs and sources of info

Nigel Fletcher for not complaining if dinner was burnt during working weekends

Malcolm Tait for keeping a delicate editorial hand on the tiller

INTRODUCTION

I became a poker addict at school, where, needless to say, gambling was illegal. Unfortunately the stakes quickly outgrew the players, and the game soon collapsed. When it resumed, we played for 'beverages' – not money, and after a very lucky run, my mornings began with the luxury of a hot coffee – delivered by a disgruntled fellow player. Poker made school bearable for me, and after years of no play, I now regard my current weekly game with all the reverence of a Sunday School.

In that time, there has been an explosion of interest. Turn on the television – at virtually any time – and you're certain to see the amazing Willie Tann knocking out one poker 'celebrity' or another. A few years ago, you'd have been ostracised for cursing a 'gay waiter', yearning for a 'German virgin' or kicking a 'dog'. Not today. You no longer need dark glasses, nicotine-stained fingers and the look of a person who's crawled out from beneath a brick to get the weird language of poker. It's everywhere. And this wonderfully entertaining book captures it all – the slang, the tips, the legends. If you're not already intrigued, you will be.

Zac Goldsmith

Zac inherited his love of poker from his father at a disturbingly young age. He still finds time to edit The Ecologist

POKER IN PROSE

Serious players are at war with the shuffle. They tend to prefer no-limit or pot-limit hold 'em because big-bet poker gives them the leverage to win pots *without* the best hand. The most talented among them don't even need a small pair to take down a pot; one large, well-timed raise, in response to some flicker of doubt in a bettor's eyes or a twinge along the side of his neck, does the trick. Latter-day maestros like Harman and Duke, Men 'The Master' Nguyen, John Juanda and Erik Seidel can deduce with mind-bending precision from your facial tics and body language, and from how you played earlier hands, what cards you hold now; they play *you* and the size of your stack as much as they play their own cards, ruthlessly taking advantage of whatever anxiety you betray about your hand. If you've raised them with anything short of the mortal nuts – those rare pocket cards that combine with the board to make up an unbeatable hand – they can feel your level of confidence *drip... drip... drip* a quarter-notch below 100 percent; and the meek won't inherit this pot.

James McManus, *Positively Fifth Street, Murderers, Cheetahs and Binion's World Series of Poker* (2003)

CARD SHARP

O, when I die, just bury me
In a box-black coat and hat,
Put a twenty-dollar gold piece on my watch chain
To let the Lord know I'm standing pat.
Eulogy to the infamous gambler 'Canada Bill' Jones (d.1877), delivered by a friend at his funeral

POKER PUZZLER

Rounders may be a popular English version of baseball,
but in terms of poker, what are 'rounders'?
(Hint: Matt Damon starred in a 1998 poker movie of the same name.)
Answer on page 153.

POKER ETIQUETTE

Although poker's image may have a swashbuckling, even crooked side, players are expected to behave in an exemplary fashion:

Swearing
Don't. No matter how annoyed you are. Poker players are supposed to be tough and cool, and not the sorts to throw their toys out of their pram just because they've lost.

Pay attention
There's nothing more annoying than someone who keeps asking whose turn it is or what the value of the chips are. If you can't focus for 10 minutes on the cards, you're not likely to make it as a poker ace, are you?

Don't delay
Although long hesitations can both give the idea that you're undecided and make other players nervous at some stages, it's not polite to take forever to decide what to do at every move – it just slows the game down for everyone.

Discarding cards
If you must flick your cards back at the dealer, do so at a moderate speed and don't aim for their hands. Alternatively, push them forward.

Play in turn
Even though you may look at your cards after the deal and know you're going to throw them in instantly, wait until it's your turn. The number of players left in does make a difference to some people's game play.

Splashing the pot
Throwing chips into the pot so they bounce all over the place and knock others about is considered rude. It also means other players can't always see what you've bet.

Stringing your bet
Some players like to fiddle with stacks of chips, taking far more than they intend to bet and drawing attention to them to make their opponents nervous or mislead them. They also add chips to the pot in small numbers to psyche out opponents. The polite way is to put your chips in, in a neat pile, in one go.

Too much information
Don't talk about the hand being played or the cards you may have thrown while the hand is still in progress. This gives an unfair advantage to some players.

Stay seated
Unless you're all in, in which case it's traditional to stand up to see the hand out, don't leave the table during a hand.

Peek-a-boo
When cards are about to be shown, don't try and see the cards of a neighbouring player until they're on the table – leaning like someone trying to eyeball a fellow commuter's newspaper is considered bad manners.

CARD SHARP

Poker is a game of people. If you remember that, you can bounce your opponents round like tumbleweeds in Texas. If you forget, Lord have mercy on your bankroll.
Doyle Brunson, poker player

AMARILLO SLIM'S BEST SIDE BETS

Apart from being one of the most skillful players the game has ever seen, Amarillo Slim certainly deserves the title of most colourful. A gambling man from head to toe, he became famous for the crazy bets he'd make with celebrities and other champions. Here are some of the best:

1. Hammered at golf
Amarillo Slim made many bets with legendary motorcycle stuntman Evel Knievel, including one that he could beat him at golf, playing only with a carpenter's hammer.

2. Down to the river
During a game with Jimmy 'The Greek' Snyder, Slim bet that he could swim down the 'river of no return' – a particularly dangerous 29-mile length of rapids in Idaho – in the middle of winter. Jacques Cousteau made him a special wet suit to keep out the cold.

3. Strike!
While playing in a back room behind a bowling alley in New Jersey, Slim was challenged by the local bowling champion. Being an indifferent bowler, Slim instead offered the champ odds if he could score more than 70 bowling

blindfold, his only caveat being that the bowler must retrieve his ball each time. As Slim knew, this is very disorientating and eventually his opponent only scored 43. Other friends, hearing about the bet, insisted it was possible. Slim took them on too, and one wound up so confused he threw his ball through the plate glass window of the alley.

4. Follow that camel
While playing in the first European Poker Championship in Casino El Mamounia in Marrakech, Slim was challenged to ride a camel through the newly refurbished hotel (King Hassan II had just spent about £50m doing it up). Once inside, the camel ran amok with Slim clinging to its back, until someone had the bright idea of fetching a female camel in heat. His infatuated mount followed her straight out.

POKER CITIES

San Francisco

Some of the biggest games of poker ever played took place in San Francisco in the years after the gold rush in that area in the mid-nineteenth century. Several private poker rooms opened in the city, the most renowned of which was the famous Cinch Room in the Palace Hotel, which was advertised as 'richly equipped with innumerable brass spittoons'. About 10 or 12 of the richest men in the West participated in these titanic battles, among them James C Flood, one of the original owners of the fabulous Big Bonanza mine in Nevada, and four state senators – James G Fair, John Percival Jones, William Sharon and William M Stewart, all of whom had made their fortunes buying and selling shares in the mines built over the renowned Comstock Lode. This group probably played for higher stakes than any other poker school in history, a $50,000 pot being common among them and one of $100,000 not unusual – the equivalent of several million dollars today. In the course of 15 years of high stakes play, Sharon alone is said to have won $1m playing poker in a single San Francisco club.

THE CONSEQUENCES OF CHEATING

Tarring and feathering is an ancient punishment, dating back at least as far as the reign of Richard the Lionheart (1189-1199). A statute of this time ordained that a convicted felon 'shal have his head shorn, and boyling pitch poured upon his head, and feathers or downe strawed upon the same, whereby he may be knowen'.

The practice was popular in America's Wild West, when it was commonly used to rid towns of crooked gamblers. It could be a severe punishment: painting hot tar onto skin caused painful blistering and when the coating was removed it often took hairs and burnt flesh with it. Because of this, tar was applied over a victim's clothes in lesser cases. In its heyday, which coincided with the railway boom, the tarring and feathering concluded with the victim being 'ridden out of town on a rail'.

Among those subjected to the punishment was Joseph Smith, the founder of Mormonism, who was tarred, feathered and forced to drink a quantity of nitric acid by a mob in Hiram, Ohio, in 1832. Mark Twain, threatened with a similar fate a few years later, replied: 'If it weren't for the honour and glory of the thing, I'd just as soon walk.'

THE POKER PRESIDENT

President Warren G Harding is regarded by most historians (especially American ones) as the worst incumbent (1921-1923) the White House has ever seen. Harding received the highest majority a president has ever managed, but within weeks of entering the White House, he had begun tarnishing its image. A bland politician who concentrated on being genial and having no opinion on anything controversial, Harding surrounded himself with a bunch of cronies from his home state of Ohio whom he appointed to important state positions. Journalists quickly came up with the tag 'the Poker Cabinet', and with 'the Ohio Gang' around him, Harding put most of his energies into ceremonial appearances and hosting all-night parties where they would drink, smoke, play poker and tell jokes into the early hours. On one occasion he gambled away all the White House china when he ran out of chips.

DISH THE DOSH

Part of colourful gambling lore is the names often given to amounts of money. Here's a quick guide to the value of marigolds, Marshalls and macaronis:

£1,000,000 – marigold
£100,000 – plum
£1,000 – cow, grand, gorilla (a big monkey), K (from kilogramme)
£500 – monkey
£200 – twoer
£150 – buck, yard-and-a-half
£100 – century, tonne, big one, C, C-note, one bill
£50 – yard
£25 – pony, macaroni (Cockney rhyming slang)
£20 – score
£10 – double-finnup, long-tailed finnup, cock and hen or cockle and hen (Cockney rhyming slang)
£5 – Abraham (Abraham Newland, chief cashier of the Bank of England, 1778 to 1807), Marshall (Matthew Marshall, chief cashier, 1835 to 1864), fin or finnup (both from Yiddish funf, meaning five), flimsy, horse, Lil (from the Romany for book), Jacks (Cockney rhyming slang from Jack's alive)

POKER IN PROSE

Not a muscle was relaxed on the part of the onlookers. Not the weight of a body shifted from one leg to the other. It was a sacred silence. Only could be heard the roaring draft of the huge stove, and from without, muffled by the log-walls, the howling of dogs. It was not every night that high stakes were played on the Yukon, and for that matter, this was the highest in the history of the country. The saloon-keeper finally spoke.

'If anybody else wins, they'll have to take a mortgage on the Tivoli.'

The two other players nodded.

'So I call, too.' MacDonald added his slip for five thousand.

Not one of them claimed the pot, and not one of them called the size of his hand. Simultaneously and in silence they faced their cards on the table, while a general tiptoeing and craning of necks took place among the onlookers. Daylight showed four queens and an ace; MacDonald four jacks and an ace; and Kearns four kings and a trey. Kearns reached forward with an encircling movement of his arm and drew the pot in to him, his arm shaking as he did so.

Daylight picked the ace from his hand and tossed it over alongside MacDonald's ace, saying:

'That's what cheered me along, Mac. I knowed it was only kings that could beat me, and he had them.

'What did you-all have?' he asked, all interest, turning to Campbell.

'Straight flush of four, open at both ends – a good drawing hand.'

'You bet! You could a' made a straight, a straight flush, or a flush out of it.'

'That's what I thought,' Campbell said sadly. 'It cost me six thousand before I quit.'

'I wisht you-all'd drawn,' Daylight laughed. 'Then I wouldn't a' caught that fourth queen. Now I've got to take Billy Rawlins' mail contract and mush for Dyea. What's the size of the killing, Jack?'

Kearns attempted to count the pot, but was too excited. Daylight drew it across to him, with firm fingers separating and stacking the markers and I.O.U.'s and with clear brain adding the sum.

'One hundred and twenty-seven thousand,' he announced. 'You-all can sell out now, Jack, and head for home.'

The winner smiled and nodded, but seemed incapable of speech.

'I'd shout the drinks,' MacDonald said, 'only the house don't belong to me any more.'

Jack London, *Burning Daylight* (1910)

*Phoebe could never work out how Justin always seemed
to know exactly what was in her hand.*

THE CARD OF DEATH

Throughout the Far East, the ace of spades is known as the 'card of death'
and regarded as extremely unlucky (a link that probably goes back to where
the history of playing cards and tarot cards meet).

In 1966, the US government instructed the US Playing Card Company of
Cincinnati to produce several million packs made up entirely of the ace
of spades to be used in the Vietnam War. Two lieutenants from the 25th Infantry Division had
suggested that dropping packs of them would spread terror among the Vietcong.

The US Playing Card Company's famous 'Bicycle' pack design was ideal for this task
because it included a picture of a woman modelled on the Statue of Freedom,
which tops the US Capitol building, regarded by the Vietcong as a goddess of death.

POKER DEATHS

Sheriff Bud Frazer

Sheriff Bud Frazer and 'Deacon' Jim Miller were best friends in Pecos, Texas. Miller served as Frazer's deputy in the lawless town until the sheriff discovered that his partner had shot dead a prisoner to cover up his own criminal activities.

The falling out was a violent one and led to the most bizarre series of gunfights recorded in Western history. Having narrowly survived one assassination attempt, Frazer decided to get his retaliation in first on the next occasion the two men met. Spotting Miller on the street one day in April 1894, he walked up to his former friend and opened fire. The sheriff's first bullet struck Deacon Jim in the chest, and the second hit him on the right arm just as he was drawing. Miller got off two wild shots with his left hand while Frazer continued to fire, hitting his deputy twice more in the chest and once in the belly.

Assuming that Miller was dead, Frazer stalked off, unaware that his enemy had adopted the precaution of wearing a steel plate under his shirt. Badly injured but alive, the former deputy crawled off to recuperate. He recovered so well that the two men fought a second wild gunfight only eight months later. This time Frazer hit his enemy four times, and once again the chest plate saved Miller's life. Legend says that Bud was unaware his target was wearing body armour and fled in terror, unable to understand how Deacon Jim could take so many solid hits.

Miller got his revenge 20 months later in the nearby town of Toyah, and it was a game of poker that did it for the sharpshooting, but none too bright, Bud Frazer. The sheriff was so caught up in the game that he failed to notice Miller sidling up to the door of his saloon. While Frazer studied his hand, his enemy placed a shotgun across the swinging doors and carefully lined up his shot. Frazer was blown in half before he could decide whether to check, raise or fold.

Jim Miller was brought to trial for murder, but acquitted when the jury decided he had done nothing to Frazer that his former friend would not have willingly done to him, given half a chance.

POKER CITIES

Cincinnati

Poker was the main game played in Cincinnati before the American Civil War. Almost every saloon in town had a poker room, many of them operated by dubious river-boat gamblers, dozens of whom spent their time staking out suckers in the city. The biggest games in town were played at the Burnet House, later famed as the spot where Ulysses S Grant and William Sherman plotted their famous 'March to the Sea'. So opulent were the fixtures and fittings at the house, and so attentive the service, that the *Illustrated London News* dubbed it 'the best hotel in the world'. Evidently the *ILN*'s correspondent hadn't been lured into a game by any of the Burnet House's crooked gamblers.

POKER IN PROSE

In his much-anthologised, tragic sketch of frontier life, Bret Harte created a classic gambling figure, Mr Oakhurst, as impenetrably calm in life as in death. Here Oakhurst explains to young Tom Simson, a boy he cleaned out then repaid, his philosophy of luck. This conversation takes place on a journey with Simson, Simson's fiancée, the old town drunkard and the local whore, all of whom have been ejected from the frontier town of Poker Flat and are facing a difficult journey to anywhere else.

At midnight the storm abated, the rolling clouds parted, and the stars glittered keenly above the sleeping camp. Mr. Oakhurst, whose professional habits had enabled him to live on the smallest possible amount of sleep, in dividing the watch with Tom Simson somehow managed to take upon himself the greater part of that duty. He excused himself to the Innocent by saying that he had 'often been a week without sleep.' 'Doing what?' asked Tom. 'Poker!' replied Oakhurst, sententiously; 'when a man gets a streak of luck, – nigger-luck, – he don't get tired. The luck gives in first. Luck,' continued the gambler, reflectively, 'is a mighty queer thing. All you know about it for certain is that it's bound to change. And it's finding out when it's going to change that makes you. We've had a streak of bad luck since we left Poker Flat – you come along, and slap you get into it, too. If you can hold your cards right along you're all right. For,' added the gambler, with cheerful irrelevance,

'"I'm proud to live in the service of the Lord, And I'm bound to die in His army."'

Bret Harte, *The Luck of Roaring Camp Suzy* (1892)

LAS VEGAS: THE EARLY YEARS

Las Vegas, at the tail end of Nevada, seems an improbable choice for gambling capital of the world. Founded in the early nineteenth century, when the rivers and springs of the Las Vegas valley made it an ideal resting place for wagon trains making their way along the Old Spanish Trail between Santa Fe and Los Angeles, its prospects of flourishing seemed so bleak that even the Mormons pulled out of the city in 1857. Two French travellers wrote at this time that the isolated settlement would 'never become considerable'.

Vegas's fortunes changed in 1905, with the arrival of the Union Pacific Railway, but it was not until the 1930s that the boom began. The population, only 945 in 1910, was still no more than 5,165 when the government decided, in the late 1920s, to build the Hoover Dam nearby. This vast project survived the Wall Street Crash to become a showpiece of Franklin Roosevelt's New Deal, employing an average of 3,500 workers with a total monthly payroll of $500,000. Much of this cash found its way back into town, and so did the 200,000 tourists who began to visit the dam each year.

With the completion of the dam, Las Vegas had to find new ways of enticing visitors. It liberalised divorce laws so that respondents who resided in town for six weeks could obtain a separation. But it was the city's determined attempts to identify itself as a tourist-friendly 'real Western town' (complete with hotels where grizzled old prospectors camped out in the lobby with mules) that really paid dividends. Gaming was legalised in 1931, and soon Las Vegas became known as the home of 'all-night gambling'. Out-of-towners with better knowledge of the casino industry soon arrived, led by the Cornero brothers – former bootleggers from California – who ran the town's first significant gambling club, The Meadows, during the 1930s. They were followed by Guy McAfee, a corrupt vice squad cop from Los Angeles in 1938, and finally by gangsters such as Bugsy Siegel after 1939.

Not even the arrival of the atomic bomb testing programme at nearby Nellis Air Force Base (400 devices were exploded there, many above ground, between 1950 and 1962) could dent the city's popularity, but America's stuttering economy certainly could. The post-war slump, which hit Las Vegas in 1947-1948, forced casinos into a ruinous price war that was finally resolved with an agreement to standardise odds and fix limits.

Only one gambler was bold enough to stand out against this conformity. Arriving in Las Vegas in 1947, Texan Benny Binion bought shares in several clubs before he opened his Horseshoe Club on Glitter Gulch in 1951. The Horseshoe offered more liberal odds and accepted higher wagers than any of its rivals, drawing high rollers from across the country to its doors. And when they got there, they wanted to play poker.

HAVE FAITH: THE SAINTS POKER PLAYERS SHOULD PRAY TO FOR A LITTLE DIVINE INTERVENTION ON THE FLOP

Against doubt
St Thomas the Apostle
(also patron saint of blind people, architects and Sri Lanka)
Against hesitation
St Joseph
(also patron saint of house hunters and the Croatian people)
Compulsive gamblers
St Bernadine of Sienna
(also patron saint of ad agencies, PR companies and chest complaints)
Las Vegas
St Peter the Apostle
(also patron saint of clock makers, butchers and people with athlete's foot)
Las Vegas (again – well, you need all the luck you can get...)
St Paul the Apostle
(also patron saint of hailstorms, snake bites and tent makers)
Good finances
Infant Jesus of Prague
(not really a saint but a statue, though the Catholic Church strenuously denies that adoration of it amounts to idolatry. People pray to the statue for family life, money and, er, good schools)

POKER PUZZLER

My first is in rogues, that you'll find at the table
And also in royals, which you'll bet on, if able.
My second's kept covered if you don't want to tell
The rest of the table you've drawn very well.
My third can be found in a regular bet
My fourth you can up, less a tiny insect.
My fifth is in fourth, in raise, and in pair
Now listen to Springsteen and he'll take you there!
What am I?
Answer on page 153.

CARD SHARP

If, after the first 20 minutes, you don't know who the sucker at the table is, it's you.
Traditional poker maxim, variously attributed to Amarillo Slim
and Paul Newman

POKER DEATHS

Stuey Ungar

Stuey Ungar, born 1953, became a professional gambler at 14. A wunderkind, he won millions at the card tables and lost them at the track. He was found dead in 1998 in a room at the Oasis Motel, South Las Vegas Boulevard, having ingested a mixture of narcotics and painkillers which triggered a pre-existing heart condition.

At the time of his death, Ungar was using coke to keep himself perky, Percodan to calm down the coke highs, and methadone, though he wasn't the first or last poker player to do so.

He won his first gin rummy tournament at 10. Shortly before he died he said that although he could conceive of there being a better poker player than him, he didn't see a better gin player coming along for another 50 years. At 15, he borrowed a $500 stake and bought his way into a big gin tournament, carrying off the $10,000 prize without ever losing a hand. He gave $1,000 to his family, the rest he lost on the horses. Dropping out of school he left New York, where he was regularly beating the city's best players two or three times his age, and headed for Miami, then the centre of high stakes gin play.

Ungar became a living legend. He could predict his opponents' hands with uncanny accuracy. When he switched to blackjack, which at the time was played with a single deck of cards, his ability to forecast the remaining cards when casino owners stopped play during his winning games led to him being banned from casino after casino. He was so good, in fact, that he couldn't get into a regular game of poker, so he was forced to play only tournaments where he could buy his way in.

Bad bets blighted his life. Even though he'd won the World Series twice by the age of 25, by 1997 he couldn't raise the money to enter and no one took him seriously. Then a benefactor paid the $10,000 entry and Ungar went on to win 10 of the 30 major no-limit hold 'em tournaments he entered in a bravura four-day show. Two months later, he was broke again, and in two days would lie dead in a cheap motel room.

MODERN CARD MARKING

Gone are the days of crudely notching cards and scratching their backs. Sophisticated technology has been brought to bear on the problem of illicitly stacking the odds in your favour. Hundreds of websites will sell you pre-marked cards and offer tips on how to use them, although they all protest the product is for magic use only.

'Glimmer' decks are marked with a special solution, which looks like a tiny smudge or natural marking, and is best detected when cards are in motion. Developed by gamblers in the 1990s, they deceived the big casinos for several years, but are very hard to learn. They cost around £35 a deck.

'Juice' is readable by the naked eye, if you're trained to spot the subtle alterations it makes to tints and lines when applied to the backs of cards. Decks are available from £60 to £70, and you can buy the secret substance for upward of £100 for a small bottle. Most of what's sold as Juice for lower prices is a less effective substitute.

'Shade' and other luminescent systems, on the other hand, add markings to the backs of cards that can only be seen using specially filtered sunglasses. Since half the poker-playing world wears sunglasses, there are many systems that focus on light filtering. A shaded deck will cost you about £40 to £50 and can sometimes be spotted by holding the cards aslant in bright light, where the marks appear like dull or burnt patches.

NAMES FOR THE BEST STARTING HANDS IN TEXAS HOLD 'EM

1. Pocket Rockets or American Airlines – two aces
2. Cowboys or King Kongs – two kings
3. Ladies – two queens
4. Big Slick – ace and king suited
5. Big Chick or Little Slick – ace and queen suited
6. Hooks or Fishhooks – two jacks
7. Royal Couple – king and queen suited
8. Blackjack or Ajax – ace and jack suited
9. Offsuit Big Slick – ace and king of different suits
10. Dimes – two 10s

BEST POKER MOVIES

Everyone's got their favourite poker showdown on screen. Whether it's the amazing realism or the sheer unlikeliness of the scenario that attracts us, there's nothing like two pairs of eyes meeting over a poker table with huge amounts at stake to crank up the tension.

The Cincinnati Kid (1965)

Lancey Howard, played by Edward G Robinson, is known as the best poker player in America. When new kid on the block Eric Stoner, played by Steve McQueen, turns up, a showdown is inevitable, and forms the climax of the film. McQueen's ice-blue stare was made for dramatic poker.

Maverick (1994)

Based on the 1960s TV series starring James Garner, this Mel Gibson vehicle is full of nods to the original, even going so far as to cast Garner as Gibson's dad. $3,000 short of his stake for a major tournament, Maverick will do anything to get his hands on some money. But he's not the only one. All sorts of card sharps and thieves are convening to play, including Mrs Annabelle Bransford, played by Jodie Foster, whose light fingers and poker face are more than a match for him.

Kaleidoscope (1966)

Warren Beatty and Susannah York bring style and realism to the poker table. Beatty's character is suave and slick, but also sly and a cheat. The gameplay is particularly accurate and gripping as he defends his title as 'the luckiest poker player ever' – presumably a reference to his tendency to cheat.

Rounders (1998)

Matt Damon is drawn back to the world of poker playing when a friend, played by Edward Norton, comes to him with a gambling debt. The film climaxes with a marathon card game as they struggle to meet the target.

Luckytown (2000)

Lidda Daniels (Kirsten Dunst) sets off for Las Vegas in search of her father, a notorious gamester played by James Caan.

Along the way she picks up video store clerk and poker wannabe, Colonel, who dreams of making it big at the casinos. On arrival she finds her father about to start a high stakes game with his old nemesis. Lots of poker scenes, and Kirsten Dunst pole dancing is a plus for the boys.

When you insist on playing cards right through dinner,
you know you're an addict.

CARD SHARP

There is no doubt that Khrushchev would have been a superb poker player. First,
he is out to win. Second, like any good poker player, he plans ahead so that he can
win the big pots. He likes to bluff, but he knows that if you bluff on small pots and
fail consistently to produce the cards, you must expect your opponent to call your
bluff on the big pots.
Richard Nixon, US President

THE WORST HAND TO DRAW

In Texas hold 'em, the hand you don't want to see when you cautiously lift up your cards is a two and a seven of different suits. They're too far apart for you to develop a straight (five cards in sequence), you have a very slim chance of picking up a flush in the next five cards (four of them would have to be one of the two suits you're holding) and even if you wind up with a pair of sevens, chances are in a game of several players, someone will have a better pair.

SLOW HAND

Probably the most praised hand ever played in the World Series of Poker was the last one dealt in the final head-to-head of 1988.

Johnny Chan, the 1987 winner, was playing against Erik Seidel of New York. Chan was the hot favourite, not least because he had nearly $1.4m in chips against Seidel's $296,000. Seidel was also considerably less experienced, having punched well above his weight even to make the final table.

Chan received J♣ 9♣, Seidel Q♣ 7♥. Both entered the pot for the minimum bet. The flop came out Q♠ 10♥ 8♦, giving Chan a concealed straight and Seidel only a pair of queens. But Chan trapped his opponent, betting only a modest $40,000 to give the impression he was holding only moderate cards. Seidel thought for a moment, and decided his high pair was well worth backing. He raised $50,000, and the cunning Chan again resisted the temptation to reveal the full strength of his hand, flat-calling. The turn brought only 2♠. Chan could not now be beaten, but again he only checked. That was enough to fool Seidel, who went all-in on his pair. The river card, 6♦, could do nothing to save him. Johnny Chan had slow-played his way to a second consecutive world title.

The hand became so celebrated that it was recreated on the silver screen. In the 1998 Matt Damon movie *Rounders*, it features as the climax of the game played between Damon and his Russian nemesis (John Malkovich).

POKER IN PROSE

Of course, the game was never played honestly, and the methods of rigging became more elaborate as the years went by. Dealing was the first element to be affected. In the early days, the deck had been dealt from a face-down position in the dealer's left hand. In 1822, an anonymous American introduced the dealing box, made of brass, half an inch longer and a little wider than the deck, covered on top with a simple thumb hole, used to push cards out through a side slit, with a spring keeping the rest in line. The open-top model came in a few years later. Soon, however, the market was deluged with rigged boxes of all sorts, with devices that in some cases can be imagined from their names: the gaff, the tongue-tell, the sand-tell, the top-sight-tell, the needle squeeze, the end squeeze, the horse box, the screw box, the coffee mill. All sorts of ingenious contraptions were fitted into these small instruments – springs, levers, sliding plates – to inform dealers of the order in advance, and to allow them to alter it invisibly and at will.

In addition to this, there were a variety of trimmed and marked cards and cards manufactured in such a way that any two could be made to stick together. What is remarkable is that these devices were all sold very openly, advertised in newspapers as 'advantage tools', and in at least one case carried on the shelves of a specialised shop around the corner from the Bowery, so that any gambler not straight from the woods would know that the chances of his being swindled were overwhelming. (Other wares included loaded dice, crooked roulette wheels, cutters and trimmers for preparing cards, poker rings for marking cards during a game, hold-outs for concealing cards in vests, sleeves and under the table, and shiners, little mirrors that enabled the artful cheater to read the hands of his opponents.) But such is the faith of the gambler. Even with these tools, adept dealing was a profession that demanded great skill, and paid accordingly. In the mid-nineteenth century, the top practitioners, known as 'mechanics' or 'artists', might make several hundred dollars a week, in addition to a cut of the profits.

Luc Sante, *Low Life: Lures and Snares of Old New York* (1991)

CARD SHARP

As elaborate a waste of human intelligence as you could find outside
an advertising agency.
Raymond Chandler on poker

THE COST OF PLAY

So you want to play like a pro. But if you want to bring the feel of tournament play to No 7 Acacia Avenue, you'll have to lay out a considerable sum to set up a professional-standard poker game. When you see the final bill it may be a case of 'read 'em and weep':

Tournament standard table for 10 players, including padded edge (tendon damage and discomfort from resting your wrists against the edge of the table is an occupational hazard for gamblers) – **£300**

Green baize cloth – **£4.99 a metre**

Lockable steel drop box (which bolts onto table so the dealer can stash away notes and chips) – **£35**

Clay composite poker chips, the old-fashioned choice, as used in most tournament play. Heavier than most chips sold for home games, they make the satisfying 'chunk' noise you hear on TV when you throw them down.
Sets of 500 'suited' – **£100 per set**

World Poker Tour standard playing cards, 12 sets – **£40**

Dealer button for Texas hold 'em – **£4**

Dealer's green visor – **£5**

Poker dice – **£2.50 for five**

POQUE, POCHSPEIL... POKER?

Lexicographers have never agreed over the origins of the word 'poker'. Early authorities on the game state that the name was derived from the French *poque*, a card game popular in Paris as early as 1700. There certainly are similarities – *poque* featured gambling on combinations of cards held in a hand, and there were several betting rounds – and the theory would also explain why poker first emerged in New Orleans, capital of the former French territory of Louisiana. But *poque*, a game played with hands of only three cards, was much less varied and subtle than poker, and the *Oxford Dictionary of Word Histories* currently favours the theory that the name originated with the German *pochspeil*, a variety of brag.

DOYLE BRUNSON'S 'READY TO PLAY' CHECKLIST

'Poker players,' says Doyle Brunson, generally reckoned to be one of the best two or three poker players ever to pick up a hand, 'would do well to examine themselves carefully before every game.' Playing in the wrong frame of mind can be an expensive mistake. Here is the checklist 'Texas Dolly' developed to test his readiness to play:

1. Have you had enough sleep? If NO, don't play.

2. Is there something else you would rather be doing? If YES, don't play.

3. Are you feeling physically well enough to sit through a movie? If NO, don't play. When you have a headache or you'd be tired or fidgety in a theatre, you probably won't play your best poker.

4. Are you so mad at someone that it's interfering with your concentration? If YES, don't play.

5. Are drugs, alcohol, or medication interfering with your logical thinking? If YES, don't play.

6. Are you emotionally upset?

If YES, don't play. Fights with your wife or girlfriend are not healthy to your money clip.

And, most important:

7. Do you feel you're going to win? If NO, don't play. Give credibility to your hidden feelings. Your subconscious might be analysing things you're not aware of.

'If it looks like a good game,' Brunson concludes, 'and you survive the checklist, then sit down and do some serious winning. Otherwise, save your energy for tomorrow.'

Doyle Brunson, *Poker Wisdom of a Champion* (1984)

POKER DEATHS

John Jenkins

Top amateur John Jenkins became one of the surprisingly few poker players to be murdered when he was shot in the back of the head in 1989. The crime was never solved, but Jenkins – who boasted of being the biggest used-book dealer in the world – had been involved in a scandal concerning forged manuscripts a few years earlier. Before his death, the part-time shark had been best known as possessor of one of the game's stranger monikers, going by the nickname 'Austin Squatty' Jenkins.

POKER PUZZLER

Which of the following is NOT a genuine poker phrase?
a) 'Don't tap on the aquarium'
b) 'My pocket aces are cracked again'
c) 'Soon I'm going to straddle the table'
d) 'He mucked his hand'
e) 'The rock raised me on the river, but I had the nuts'
Answer on page 153.

DO THE NUMBERS

At the beginning of 2003, there were an estimated 87,000 playing poker online in the UK. Quite a lot, you might think. But by 2005, the figure had risen to 1.8 million, a twenty-fold increase and then some.

Dripping sweat onto your chips is considered poor manners in any game – and a bit of a giveaway!

29

POKER GIFTS

Here is a selection of poker goodies it may never have occurred to you to try and buy (for very good reason!):

1. Poker cocktail shaker

Plastic, with club, heart, spade and diamond design. $8 (£4.50 approx).
www.go-kat-go.com

2. Casino keyring

If you can't bear to stop playing poker while doing other unnecessary things, like driving, then this is for you. Twiddle to your heart's content for only £4.99.
www.drinkstuff.com

3. Kosher chocolate poker chips

Don't use if playing with nervous people whose hands sweat a lot. $18 (£10.50 approx) for 120.
www.honestfoods.com

4. Bikini-watchers poker chip set

500 9g regulation poker chips – with a semi-naked woman in the middle. The grown-up version of *Playboy* playing cards. Of course, you could combine the two. £59.99 – yeah, baby, yeah!
www.drinkstuff.com

5. Poker-card stunts DVD

The only poker-card stunt worth learning is how to win every time, not how to flip cards about – sheesh. But if you must, another DVD teaches you all sorts of neat tricks to do with your chips, too. £19.99 each.
www.drinkstuff.com

RUNNING MAN

Super-fit poker ace Ted Forrest once accepted a $7,000 wager from fellow player Mike Svobodny that he could not complete a marathon on the University of Nevada, Las Vegas running track on the 4th of July. During the run, the temperature rose to more than 110°F and the UNLV track – red rubber-urethane – radiated heat. The first 14 miles were OK, but Forrest said later: 'The next six were a lot tougher. And the last six? It wasn't even human.' Forrest made it in the end, but only after the skin from the sole of one foot separated and came off in his sock.

The gambler believes he ended up running 108 laps of the track, not 106, because he was suffering from heat exhaustion, lost count and could no longer think clearly enough to make himself stop. 'It was two weeks before I felt human again. Today, I wouldn't take that bet for $100,000,' Ted concludes.

CALCULATING ODDS

You may need to take a calculator to the table to use this one. According to Frank Wallace, author of *The Advanced Concepts of Poker* (1968), the best way of calculating whether or not to play any given hand is to resolve the following equation:

$$\frac{\textbf{Potential size of pot x probability of winning pot}}{\textbf{Potential loss}} = \textbf{investment odds}$$

Play hands that possess investment odds of one or more and fold those that don't. Thus if a player estimates that a pot is worth around £200, that he has a one-in-four chance of winning it, and that the cost of playing the hand is £30, the equation is:

$$\frac{200 \times 0.25}{30} = 1.66$$

POKER CITIES

Atlantic City

Until 1976, if you wanted to play poker in a casino in America, you had to go to Nevada. Then the state of New Jersey earmarked the rundown coastal resort of Atlantic City for casino building and by 1985, 10 huge gambling palaces had sprung up, bringing in revenues of around $2bn.

In its heyday in the late 1980s, 80% of visitors were daytrippers who came mostly for the slots, which brought in 60% of the casinos' revenues. Although the gaming tables have much better odds, and poker is potentially even more remunerative, they have always been secondary to the slots in Jersey. But by 1990, the novelty was wearing off – punters were deserting the casinos and, by the first half of the 1990s, several had gone bust. Even Donald Trump had trouble keeping the Taj Mahal out of the red.

The future history of Atlantic City gambling is likely to be heavily influenced by the personal feud between Trump, whose properties have brought in just under a third of the city's total gambling revenues, and Steve Wynn who, along with several other Vegas moguls, is said to have his eye on the east coast's potential Vegas.

MOST MONEY FINISHES (TO 2004)

In poker it's not just the winning, and it's certainly not the taking part that counts – it's finishing in the money. Players can spend a career not winning, but placing highly, and still making an extremely good living for themselves. Here are the people who've graced the finals table at the World Series of Poker most often:

Berry Johnston	44	Johnny Chan	31	Doyle Brunson	24
TJ Cloutier	41	Tom McEvoy	29	Scotty Nguyen	20
Men Nguyen	40	Dewey Tomko	28	David Chiu	16
Phil Hellmuth	40	Erik Seidel	28	Stuey Ungar	16
Humberto Brenes	32	John Bonetti	26	Brad Daugherty	15
Chris Ferguson	32	Jack Keller	25	Mansour Matloubi	15
Jay Heimowitz	31	Huck Seed	25		

MOVIE TALK

Often characters in films say the things you wish you'd come up with during a poker game. Read and remember...

1. 'If we shoot him, we won't have anyone to play with.' – James Stewart to Arthur Kennedy on what to do when they catch the only guy playing poker with them cheating, *Cheyenne Autumn* (1964)

2. 'Is this a game of chance?' 'Not the way I play it, no.' – Opponent to WC Fields, *My Little Chickadee* (1940)

3. 'That's what it's all about, doing the wrong thing at the right time.' – *The Cincinnati Kid* (1965)

4. 'A deck of cards is like a woman... when you pick one up, you wish you hadn't.' – *Flame of the Barbary Coast* (1945)

5. 'When your opponent is holding all the aces, there's only one thing to do. Kick over the table.' – *Robin and the Seven Hoods* (1964)

6. 'How did you know he was bluffing?' 'He kept looking back at his hole cards. If you got it, you don't need to keep looking back to see what you got.' – *The Gambler from Natchez* (1954)

POKER MAGAZINES

Poker Chips, the first title devoted to the game, was launched in New York in 1896. Edited by Frederic C Finch of Manhattan and John Trevor of – somewhat improbably – Rulow, Macclesfield, the journal's content consisted solely of feeble poker anecdotes and it closed down after publishing only a couple of issues. Since then, the publishing industry has developed a stronger grasp of what poker players actually want to read, and the market for card mags has exploded. Here are five of the best titles currently available:

1. *Card Player*
Probably the most renowned poker magazine in the world, *Card Player* boasts the best tournament results service, contributors such as Johnny Chan and TJ Cloutier, and a successful online edition at www.cardplayer.com. Content assumes a detailed knowledge of poker: one recent feature was snappily entitled 'The Implied Odds Problem – utilising the concept of implied odds in making a calling decision'. Fortnightly, $99.95 (£57.50 approx) for 26 issues from *Card Player Magazine*, PO Box 8436, Red Oak, IA 51591-1436, USA.

2. *Poker Europa*
Distributed free to 200 European card rooms and casinos, *Poker Europa* aims to be the continent's No 1 card magazine. Published monthly from that well-known poker hotbed, Torquay, *Poker Europa* subscriptions cost £50 for 12 issues from 33 Parkhurst Road, Torquay TQ1 4EW, UK.

3. *Native American Casino*
First with all the latest reservation news, this highly specialist business-to-business title targets Native Americans working in the casino industry. *NAC* has a monthly circulation in excess of 30,000 and a readership that includes tribal councils as well as casino management. Subscriptions $122.75 (£70.50 approx) for 12 issues from 1446 Front Street, Suite 200, San Diego, CA 92101, USA.

4. *Gambling Times*
The granddaddy of gambling titles, launched in the 1970s, Las Vegas's own *Gambling Times* appears monthly and covers not just cards, but every sort of gambling and the casino industry in general. $38 (£22 approx) for 12 issues from Gambling Times, PO Box 91928, Long Beach, CA 90809-1928, USA.

5. *Journal of Gambling Studies*
'An interdisciplinary forum for the dissemination of information on the many aspects of gambling behaviour, both controlled and pathological,' is how this one's described. Don't panic, though – we're assured that articles are of interest to the professional and layperson alike. Quarterly, price on application, from Springer GmbH, Auslieferungs-Gesellschaft, Haberstr. 7, 69126 Heidelberg, Germany.

THE DRESS CODE

It was Elijah Skaggs, the prince of nineteenth-century card sharps and perhaps the most crooked gambler ever to operate south of the Mason-Dixon line, who first attired himself in what became the American gambler's regulation garb. Skaggs's elaborate and costly outfit was considered exceedingly elegant by contemporaries. 'He appeared in Nashville,' crime historian John Morris wrote, 'dressed in frock coat and pants of black broadcloth, a black silk vest, and patent leather boots, a white shirt with standing collar, and around his neck was wound a white choker, while, resting on his cranium, was a black stove-pipe hat, which completed his attire.'

POSH PLAYERS

John Aspinall, whose CV included gambling and zoo-keeping, was a colourful throwback to a time when the ruling classes really did rule. Born in India in 1924, when he died aged 76 he still believed the chief function of women was to 'serve the dominant male', and that 'a bout of beneficial genocide' was all that was needed to put Britain back on sound financial footing.

Expelled from Rugby for idleness, he didn't last long at Oxford or in the Royal Marines either, and legend has it that he faked a fainting fit during a major military exercise so he could attend the Ascot Gold Cup. He certainly had a talent for gambling, however, and up until the 1960 Gaming Act made gambling legal in the UK, held various floating card games around Belgravia

for his wealthy friends. In 1962, Aspinall founded the Clermont Club in Mayfair where the well-heeled lined up to play high-stakes poker. Other founder members included Sir James Goldsmith and Lord Lucan. He sold the club 13 years later to fund his other great passion, animal welfare, using the spoils to open two private zoos: Howletts and Port Lympne.

Over the years Aspinall remained in the news, first when his friend Lord Lucan went missing and then in connection with a series of keepers' deaths at his zoos. His policy of encouraging close bonding between man and animal was often decried, but he stuck with the idea, memorably stating: 'I would happily sacrifice the lives of my loved ones if that meant saving an endangered species.'

CARDS ON FILM

What is it with films called *Poker* – why have so many been named after our favourite card game? Since the silent era, no less than nine movies have been made with 'poker' as their title. Counting backwards we have:

Poker (2001)
Directed, written by and starring Vinci Vogue Anzlovar.
Slovakian film about a 'modern-day anti-hero' called Borat.

Poker (1997)
Directed by Bryn Prior and written by Rebecca Gray, who both play lead characters, along with Shanah S Blevins, Darrow Carson and Chantal Marcks.
Well-regarded character study made on a low budget. Five friends meet to play five card stud... one of them is dying of cancer.

Poker (1996)
Black-and-white short, written and directed by Randy Gordon.

Poker (1992)
Short film, written and directed by Gaspar Hernandez III, about poker buddies who meet in a remote cabin and are menaced by aliens.

Poker (1988)
Thriller written and directed by Catherine Corsini, about a woman who loves playing big stakes poker against men, but runs into trouble when she plays her boss.

Poker (1970)
TV movie, directed by Chris Betz, translated by Willy van Hemert from Reginald Rose's play, made in Belgium, in Dutch.

Poker (1951)
Written and directed by Gösta Bernhard, in Swedish.

Poker (1920)
Silent cartoon, produced by the Fleischer Brothers, also known as *The Card Game*.

Poker (1913)
Silent cartoon, written and directed by Emile Cohl.

CARD SHARP

The poker player learns that sometimes both science and common sense are wrong; that the bumblebee can fly; that, perhaps, one should never trust an expert; that there are more things in heaven and earth than are dreamt of by those with an academic bent.
David Mamet, playwright

'How can three sweet old ladies have run up quite this many IOUs?'

POKER PUZZLER

You have the ace and king of spades. Your only opponent has a pair of aces. On the flop and the turn the queen and jack of spades have come up, along with the seven and six of hearts. What is your chance of winning on the river?

a) 7%
b) 27%
c) 47%
d) 67%

Answer on page 153.

POKER CITIES

New Orleans

During the first years of the nineteenth century, gambling flourished more fully in New Orleans than in any other town or city in North America. Commercial gambling was permitted there, and as early as 1810, it was reported to be home to as many gambling halls as the four largest American cities put together. It was in these places that the game of poker was born.

Poker appealed to the professional card sharps who haunted both New Orleans and the Mississippi river boats because it could be run either as a banking game, in which the dealer's income came from percentages fixed in their favour or, in more favourable circumstances, as a private game in which the sharp's dubious skills assured him of a profit.

Poker's real origins can be traced to 'the Swamp' – as the New Orleans waterfront was known – where numerous gambling 'infernos' offered the game. Few, if any, were on the level and almost all were infested with card sharps, most of them operating in teams of three. In such cases, one person dealt the cards, one sought out potential players and the third acted as a shill, apparently winning huge sums in high-stakes hands. One travellers' guide to the territory warned its readers that 'gaming adventurers' and 'black legs' were 'the lowest class of people' in the Mississippi Valley.

Many of the sharps' earliest victims were boatmen who made the arduous voyage down the Mississippi on rafts loaded with cargoes for the port. By the late 1820s, however, when the English actor Joseph Cowell made the same journey on a river boat, a trip down the river meant 'an uncontrolled yearly opportunity for the young merchants and their clerks to go it with perfect looseness, mixed up indiscriminately with vagabonds of all nations who then made New Orleans their jumping-off place.'

WATCH THE BIRDIE

In 1998, Doyle Brunson was lured back onto the golf course for the first time in years to take part in a poker champions' foursome, partnering Mike Sexton against Huck Seed and Howard Lederer. The older men were permitted to tee off from the women's tees, but Brunson had practised intensively for a week and surprised the opposition with the quality of his play. He holed a 35-foot putt at the 16th to unnerve Seed and Lederer, and he and Sexton won the $336,000 match by a stroke. According to Brunson, the largest golf bet he ever took was for around $400,000.

POKER IN PROSE

During the mid-nineteenth century, the lethal dangers of protracted poker marathons were as taken for granted as the dire consequences of self-abuse – as the reformed gambler Jonathan Green explained:

Sometime in the year 1835, in the city of New Orleans, there happened at one of its haunts of gambling, several of that unfortunate class of men who are addicted to that vice; and having large amounts of money in their possession, there was a proposition that five of the most monied men among them should sit at play until their money was exhausted. The five began, and played on, under the influence of great excitement, for some 30 hours, when two of the party quit, either from the want of money or strength. The other three continued for some 15 hours longer, when one of them had to quit also. The other two played on about 10 hours more, when one of them dropped to sleep, and this broke up the game. But next came the dreadful consequences of this rash and wicked undertaking. One of this party lived, when at home, somewhere eastward; another lived in Alexandria, on Red River; a third lived in Cincinnati; a fourth, in or near Covington, Kentucky; and the fifth near Lawrenceburg, Iowa, and this last is the only one that now survives of that unfortunate party. The eastern man was, from the time of this desperate act, afflicted, and died of disease of the lungs in '37 or '38. The one from Alexandria survived, I think, until the year '39 or '40. The one from Covington became, from that time, the subject of sore affliction, and lingered along until the year '42, when he died, having suffered more than it is in the power of language to describe. He died a sincere convert to Christianity, and was buried in the Methodist graveyard, near Covington... The fourth one of these young men died in Cincinnati in the year 1842... One other still survives, and is yet pursuing the odious practice of gambling, and most sincerely do I desire that, ere it is too late, he may take into serious consideration the many risks he is running of not being so fortunate as the last two mentioned in the narrative. (For as I have never learned the particulars of the death of the two first, I cannot give any information of their last days that would be definite or satisfactory.)

JH Green, *An Exposure of the Arts and Miseries of Gambling* (1843)

POKER DEATHS

'Wild Bill' Hickok

James Butler Hickok – better known as 'Wild Bill' – was a gunman who, owing to the well-known dangers of playing cards in Western saloons, always insisted on sitting with his back to the wall. On 2 August 1876, however, Bill was enticed into a poker game at Carl Mann's Number Ten Saloon in Deadwood, South Dakota. Hickok's favourite seat had been taken by Charlie Rich, a gambler who, to tease his friend, refused to give it up. 'Wild Bill' sat instead with his back to the rear door.

In the course of the afternoon, a nobody by the name of 'Crooked Nose' Jack McCall entered the saloon and crept up behind the gunman, shooting him once in the back of the head with his .45 revolver. Hickok's body jerked forward; then he toppled backwards off his stool. The hand he was holding when he died was an excellent one: a pair of aces and a pair of eights with a jack kicker (some say the fifth card was a queen).

McCall gave various reasons for shooting 'Wild Bill', claiming at one time that he and his victim had argued in a card game (which was never proved) and at another that Hickok had killed his brother (McCall had no brother). Possibly the murder was motivated simply by a desire for fame. In any case, the killer was cleared of murder by an illegal 'miner's court' immediately after the shooting, only to be brought to trial in Yankton, the territory's capital, a few months later. Found guilty, McCall was hanged on 1 March 1878 and buried with the rope still around his neck.

Ever since Hickok's untimely end, aces over eights have been known as the Dead Man's Hand.

CARD SHARP

Always remember, the first thing a gambler has to do is make friends with himself. A lot of people go through this world thinking they're someone else. There are a lot of players sitting at this table with mistaken identities. You wouldn't believe it.
Former world poker champ 'Puggy' Pearson

POKER FOOD

The Sandwich

Sandwiches and gambling go hand in hand, and legend has it that it was the Earl of Sandwich who created the most eaten lunch in Britain. In 1762, the Earl, a serious gambler, was playing cards with the royal set and, deep in a game, told a servant to bring him some meat between two pieces of bread so he could pick it up easily and eat it while continuing to play. His card partners soon began asking for food 'like Sandwich' as well, as there was very little the nobility of the day were more devoted to than long and intense card games. The tradition has continued, and sarnies are the most common form of food served while playing poker at home, after crisps and nuts.

The current Earl of Sandwich, John Montague, runs a catering franchise making, you guessed it, upper-crust sandwiches. Among the varieties available from the snappily (and logically) named company, Earl of Sandwich, is the Hawaiian (created with the Sandwich Islands in mind), containing barbecue pork, pineapple and Swiss cheese. We're not sure how authentically 'Sandwich Island' the cheese is, mind you...

BEST BET FOR RETIRED GAMBLERS

Fifteen places for card players to settle down:
Diamond Creek, Victoria, Australia
Forth Bridge, Fife, Scotland
Ace River, Carolina, USA
Chip Lake, Alberta, Canada
Jackpot, Nevada, USA
River, Sussex, England
Poker Street, Wismar, Guyana
Deal, Kent, England
King Island, Victoria, Australia
Four Ladies Bank, Antarctica
Luck, Zimbabwe
Fortune Hill, Newfoundland, Canada
Spade, Texas, USA
Hearts Hill, Saskatchewan, Canada
Chance City (now a ghost town), New Mexico, USA

TOP WOMEN EARNERS

The day a woman wins the World Series of Poker, Amarillo Slim is reported to have said he will eat his hat. Knowing Amarillo, he will have one woven out of spun sugar or baked as a cake. Although there are no women in the WSOP Millionaires Club, some female players have made millions. Here are the top money-earners in the game:

1. Annie Duke $3,136,221
2. Kathy Liebert $1,995,177
3. Jennifer Harman $1,425,139
4. Lucy Rokach...$955,472
5. Nani Dollinson...$710,211
6. 'Mimi' Tran Thi Thi...$675,712
7. Cyndy Violette $657,904
8. Barbara Enright..$468,868
9. Xuyen 'Bad Girl' Pham...$416,379
10. Tiffany Williamson $400,000

POKER AND THE BOMB

Just before the end of the Second World War, US President Harry S Truman took a few days' rest on board the *USS Augusta*. He spent the voyage playing poker in the company of members of the White House press corps, play starting at 8.30am and continuing until midnight. Eventually, Secretary of State James Byrnes asked United Press reporter Merriman Smith: 'Why in the world don't you leave the President alone?'

'Leave him alone?' Smith replied. 'We don't start these games, he does.'

It was while on board the *Augusta* that Truman first revealed the existence of the atomic bomb, explaining to his poker buddies from the press its history, development and intended use over Hiroshima. The briefing was arranged for 8am so that the players could ante up and deal promptly, as usual, at 8.30am.

SONGS FOR GAMBLERS

'The Winner Takes it All'..Abba
'Do You Dare Make a Bet with Amarillo Slim?'........................John 'Lutz' Ritter
'Kentucky Gambler'...Dolly Parton
'Deacon Blue'..Steely Dan
'Gambler's Blues'...Otis Rush
'Cincinnati Kid'..Prince Buster
'Tumbling Dice'...Rolling Stones
'Free Money'...Patti Smith
'Gambling'...Roots Radics
'Long Shot Kick de Bucket'...The Pioneers
'You Never Get Too Big and You Sure Don't Get Too Heavy That
You Don't Have to Stop and Pay Some Dues Sometime'...........................Doug Sahm

POKER FOOD

The Poker Party

In the 1950s and 1960s, when hostesses seemed to spend a lot of time fluttering around worrying about matching napkins and making themed food out of spam and tinned peas, cooks like Marguerite Patten were offering advice on how to make novelty sandwiches. What could be more appropriate for card-party refreshment than sandwiches cut in the shapes of the suits?

Patten's seminal *A-Z of Cookery in Colour*, from 1963, says sandwiches need never be dull, and advises fresh bread, a moist filling and pressing the two sides together firmly before cutting out with a novelty pastry cutter. For garnish, mandarin oranges and cocktail onions are offered (not necessarily together), while fillings consist mostly of anything minced with mayonnaise and flavoured soft cheese. Then there's the lambs' brains, walnut, salad dressing and mustard combo... If you're feeling more robust, then the mashed baked bean, pickled onion, Worcestershire sauce and bacon toastie might be more your thing.

Card-shaped pastry cutters can still be purchased, from http://store.everyday-essentials.co.uk, for just £5 a set. The rest is up to you...

KING OF THE RIVER BOATS

The greatest river-boat gambler of all time was George H Devol, an Ohio native who played poker, faro and rondo up and down the Mississippi for more than four decades, winning, it was estimated, more than a million dollars over the years.

Devol was the son of a ship's carpenter and his father was often away from home. Growing up largely free of any restraining influences, young George was a bad student and often in trouble at school. Running away from home at the age of 10, he got a job on a river steamer as a cabin boy and soon began to pick up the rudiments of various card games. By the time he was 15, he was a fine bluffer and an expert at 'seven-up' poker. He was also mastering the arts of card sharping, learning how to deal seconds, palm cards, stock decks and recover the cut.

In the mid 1840s, Devol travelled south to where the US was fighting Mexico in Texas. He used his new-found skills to cheat numerous soldiers out of their pay and headed home at the age of 17 with a bankroll of nearly $3,000. From there he worked his way back along the Mississippi in the company of other noted card cheats of the era such as 'Big Alexander' and 'Canada Bill' Jones.

Devol played many games of high-stakes poker against ministers, and would always return their money to them when he'd cleaned them out with the warning: 'Go and sin no more.' But he exhibited no such scruples when playing against the farmers, businessmen and soldiers who thronged the river boats.

In the 1870s, Devol branched out, travelling extensively in the Wild West in search of action. He played high-stakes games on trains – on one occasion cleaning out one of the directors of the railroad he was riding on, with the unfortunate result that the outraged official prohibited all future gaming on his trains.

Devol finally retired from gambling, aged 67, in 1896. He spent his remaining years selling copies of his memoirs, *Forty Years a Gambler on the Mississippi*, but like so many professional poker players of the era, his losses more than matched his winnings over time and he was all but penniless when he died.

POKER IN PROSE

Writing about a year spent playing poker professionally, Anthony Holden describes the weird twilight in which poker players exist by highlighting the Malta leg of the European Poker Championships.

Carved in stone above the entrance to the casino (and no doubt post-dating the Papal Knight's summer evenings) was a Latin inscription proclaiming DEUS NOBIS HAEC OTIA FECIT. What odds would I get against being the world's only poker pro with a classical education? No bets were taken as I offered a literal English rendering – 'God created these delights for us' – and then translated into American: 'Gambling is the brainchild of the Lord'.

This seemed to go down well enough with everyone except the casino staff, who were used to knowing more about gaming operations than their customers, and the long-suffering employees of the adjacent Dragonara Hotel, who were evidently used to keeping fairly regular hours. Even the 'born-again' contingent, surprisingly numerous among the world's leading poker players, are accustomed to ordering a pastrami on rye – wherever they may be in the world – at four o'clock in the morning. And they expect it to arrive before noon.

For reasons no one can satisfactorily explain, poker is essentially an act of darkness. By which I mean that it feels odd to play poker in daylight. To professionals abroad, bereft of the timelessness of Las Vegas, and used to casinos which close at dawn, it thus becomes the norm to play by night and sleep by day. One interesting socio-medical consequence of this is that it is very rare, on either side of the Atlantic, to hear a poker player complaining of jet lag.

The Maltese, however, are not used to visitors ignoring their sunshine – especially in November, when this rare commodity is the only conceivable reason for visiting their island (which otherwise put me in mind of a giant, disused Second World War aircraft hanger). The Dragonara, therefore, had made no provision for the ordering of blueberry pancakes between the hours of midnight and 6am. As this is one of the few time intervals per day when most American gamblers feel the need for such refreshment, many of them had already checked out of the Dragonara, used their 'funny money' to rent 'dipshit' automobiles, and hied themselves off to the homeliness of the distant Hilton – where, even in Malta, waffles at dawn raise few eyebrows. The Brits, of course, were happy where they were, partly because the bacon, eggs and chips were still available at lunchtime, and partly because the Dragonara was significantly less expensive.

Anthony Holden, *Big Deal* (1990)

CARD SHARP

Cards are war, in disguise of a sport.
Charles Lamb in *Essays of Elia* (1832)

THE HOUSE WITH THE BRONZE DOOR

In the United States, when gambling was enjoying one of its most glittering heydays during the sybaritic 'Gilded Age' (1870-1895), poker and games of chance were nonetheless illegal. Gaming-house owners got around this problem by turning their premises into private members' clubs, which the police were forbidden to enter without due cause. Fearsome bouncers kept a weather eye out for plain-clothes detectives, but it was always thought advisable to fit a club with a stout door capable of withstanding a police raid long enough to allow any eminent guests to make themselves scarce through a rear exit. The wealthy gambler Frank Farrell outdid all his competitors in this respect when he remodelled a famous club that had opened on Manhattan's West 33rd Street in 1891. In addition to spending $480,000 on the most opulent fixtures and furnishings, Farrell's architect, Stanford White, installed a wrought-iron door weighing several hundred pounds at the front entrance and spent an additional $20,000 on a still heavier bronze door that guarded the inner sanctums of the club. This bronze door, White claimed, had been unearthed in Italy, where in 1498 it had guarded the entrance to the Doge's wine cellars in Venice. 'The House with the Bronze Door', as it soon became known, traded vastly profitably for a decade and was never successfully raided by the police.

GO TO HELL

New York newsman Herbert Swope was notorious for the ruses he used to distract his poker buddies at critical moments. Shortly after dawn one morning in the late 1920s, when politician Bernard Baruch was down a huge sum and was desperate to keep the game going to recoup his losses, a servant entered the room, saying: 'Mr Baruch, I have the President on the line for you.' Suspecting Swope had planned the interruption to break up the session, Baruch snarled: 'Tell the President to go to hell!' Unfortunately for him, the call was genuine and Calvin Coolidge was distinctly unamused.

THE ORIGINS OF STUD

Stud poker dates back to around the year 1880, and many unlikely stories are told to explain how the game first got its name. Among the most implausible is the one proposed by George Fisher, author of the *Stud Poker Blue Book, the Only Standard Authority* (1934), who records that this version of the game originated in 'a backwoods saloon' in 'the region of Ohio' as far back as the late 1860s. On one occasion, Fisher says a group of desperadoes sat down to a game of draw poker, and after a while played a hand in which one of the participants drew three kings. Two other gamblers stayed with him through several rounds of raises, and the opener, having already bet all the money he had, rushed outside to the hitching post and led his horse, a fine stallion, into the saloon.

The guilty looks on his opponents' faces told their own story when the man returned. 'You fellows know damned well what I'm betting on,' the gambler declared, 'and I've got all my money up on it. Now I propose that, to make it fair all round, each man turns three of his cards face up, discards two and draws two more face down. I'll gamble this here studhorse *on my* chances.'

POKER DEATHS

Buster Keaton

When much-loved silent comedian Buster Keaton contracted lung cancer, after years of smoking, his family and friends for some reason hid the reality from him and told him instead that he was having a bout of chronic bronchitis. Keaton eventually died on 1 February 1966, following a seizure the previous afternoon, while he was engaged in playing poker with friends at his home in Hollywood.

Keaton was best known for his deadpan expression and the comic genius of films like *The General* and *Sherlock Jr* in the 1920s, but he also made a comeback in the 1950s. Born Joseph Frank Keaton, he got his nickname from the famous escapologist Harry Houdini, who watched him fall down a flight of stairs as a toddler and exclaimed: 'What a buster your kid took!' He began his career before he was even a year old in his parents' vaudeville act and, apart from a brief stint in the armed forces during the First World War, when he was a cryptographer, he performed all his life.

Given the choice he would probably have died on set but, all in all, going out during a poker game doesn't seem like the worst way for it to end.

SEVEN NOVICE MISTAKES AT FACE-TO-FACE PLAY

Everyone has to start somewhere... but for a jaded poker crowd, new players are fish to be hooked, greenhorns to clear out. Over and over they've seen you and I make the same mistakes and are always looking out for them, eager to take advantage:

1. Not knowing how much to bet Novices often hesitate about putting in a large bet at an early stage.

2. Getting worn down With a limited stake, some novices don't like to play risky hands and tend to fold too easily, with their money being worn away gradually, hand by hand, so when they do get a good hand they don't have half as much to throw at it.

3. Acting over-casual Those new to face-to-face poker often don't know how to act and, when faced with a great draw, try too hard to conceal their excitement.

4. Looking at the cards too much After the draw, if a novice has something good they often go back and look at it, like they can't help themselves. If they act out of pattern other players will notice.

5. Acting nervously Everyone else at the table is watching for any pattern in their behaviour – the tiniest twitch or the slightest repetition.

6. Confusing luck with skill The over-confident newcomer may presume luck is against them when they lose a lot. It could just be being outplayed, but their ego won't let them consider that.

7. Deep pockets Novices often don't see which way play is running and, in no-limits games, get carried away with the betting. If you're losing, it's 90% down to you being outclassed. Decide how much to risk and stick to it.

POKER PUZZLER

In which of the following poker variants do you not have to use any of the cards dealt you to make up your final hand?

a) Seven-card stud high/low

b) Two-card manila

c) Three-card manila

d) Omaha high/low split

Answer on page 153.

They say the best way to hide something is in plain view...
but in the case of guns it's just plain off-putting to other players.

10 POKER PROS WHO PLAY ONLINE

Player	Who's that?	Online nickname
Peter Costa	2003 Crown Australian Champion	The Poet
Steve Badger	Poker writer	ThunderRoad
David Colclough	WSOP final tables	le cerveau
'Miami' John Cernuto	WSOP bracelet winner	Miami John
Barbara Enright	WSOP ladies event winner	ItsOnlyMe
Kirill Gerasimov	2002 World Heads Up champion	Krill
Randy Holland	WSOP bracelet winner	razzman99
Cy Jassinowsky	British Open NLHE winner	Piesang
Chris Moneymaker	WSOP 2003 winner	Moneymaker
John Vorhaus	Poker writer	KillerPoker

THE REAL GOTHAM CITY

By the end of the nineteenth century, illegal gambling – fuelled by the fast-rising popularity of poker – underpinned the economy of one of the most corrupt cities the world has ever known. The Democrats, based at Tammany Hall, held power in New York almost without break from the 1850s until 1914, funding their awesome political machine with the proceeds of vice. Brothels, illicit after-hours drinking dens and gambling houses all made regular monthly protection payments to the city's politicians, receiving in return an unwritten licence to operate their businesses. The police, far from clamping down on these illegal activities, acted as collectors of protection for their masters. Much of the money gathered in this way was used to bribe voters and fix elections, thus perpetuating the system.

By the time *The New York Times* exposed the outrage in March 1900, Tammany's total revenues from gambling alone exceeded $3m a year, made up as follows:

Pool rooms, 400 at $300 a month	$1,440,000
Crap games, 500 at $150 a month	$900,000
Small gambling houses, 200 at $150 a month	$360,000
Large gambling houses, 20 at $1,000 a month	$240,000
Envelope games*, 50 at $50 a month	$30,000
Policy**	$125,000
Total	$3,095,000

*'Envelope' games were pawnshop swindles that involved customers bidding for sealed envelopes containing unredeemed pawn tickets. Naturally no one ever found the tickets that would have redeemed the more lucrative objects on display inside their envelopes.

**'Policy' was a form of lottery, generally organised out-of-state and frequently rigged.

POKER NATION

By 2005, the number of poker players in the United States had passed the 50-million mark – nearly one-fifth of the population. The TV-fuelled boom has drawn tens of millions of new players to the game since the year 2000, almost a third of them women.

WHAT'S THE CHANCE OF THAT?

In a full deck of cards there are only so many of each type of hand you could possibly get when playing five-card draw poker, or 'classic' poker as it's sometimes called. There are 2,598,960 possible combinations of the 52 cards in a deck, which allows one to calculate the odds of any five being drawn. Here are your chances of being dealt every possible hand – just to give you an idea of what you're up against.

Hand	Number of possible hands in deck	Odds against
Royal flush	Four	649,739:1
Straight flush	40	64,973:1
Four of a kind	624	4,164:1
Full house	3,744	693:1
Flush	5,108	508:1
Straight	10,200	254:1
Three of a kind	54,912	46:1
Two pair	123,552	20:1
One pair	1,098,240	1.25:1
No pair	1,302,540	Evens

POKER POOCH PAINTINGS

Millions of people are familiar with the work of Cassius Marcellus Coolidge, but hardly any of them know his name. Coolidge was the painter of the original 'dogs playing poker' scenes that became kitsch classics. Coolidge originally painted just nine scenes of anthropomorphised animals sitting at play for a Minnesota advertising company in 1903, two of which were sold recently at the Doyle Auction House, New York, for $590,400.

As well as bequeathing us this poker classic, Coolidge was the inventor of those comedy figures with holes cut out for the head that you see at funfairs, and also managed to found a bank and a newspaper during his busy life.

THE SCIENCE OF BLUFF: DR RIDDLE AND THE POKER SCHOOL

Poker has been the subject of more than one PhD thesis, but perhaps the most eccentric is *Aggressive Behaviour in a Small Social Group*, a pioneering psychological study conducted by one Ethel M Riddle during the 1920s. Riddle wired six poker players up to lie detectors during a game of five-card stud and studied the stimulus her players received when examining their own cards or analysing those revealed by opponents. She used the data gathered to show that poker players are poor judges of the bluff, overestimating the number of attempts at bluffing by infrequent bluffers and underestimating the attempts of the frequent bluffer.

Riddle's eventual conclusion was that players maximise their chances of success if they bluff precisely 6% of the time.

CARD SHARP

There is a very easy way to leave a casino with a small fortune.
Go there with a large one.
Jack Yelton, realist

STUEY UNGAR, CARD COUNTER

Stuey Ungar is remembered as one of the most gifted, if not *the* most gifted, player – not just of poker but of gin rummy and countless other card games – that the world has ever seen. Part of his skill was down to his amazing card-counting ability and mathematical brain that allowed him to figure out the most amazing odds.

In the mid 1970s, banned from most casinos because he was too good and kept beating the house, Ungar bet any takers that he could count down the last two decks in a six-deck card shoe from which games were dealt, having seen the first four decks worth of cards removed. Despite offering to wager $10,000 on the feat, no one wanted a piece of his action, but Bob Stupak – former owner of Vegas World and designer of the Stratosphere Tower – offered him $100,000 to his $10,000 if he could do something even more amazing: count the last three decks out of six.

It sounds impossible, but Ungar counted down 156 cards, not missing a single one, and claimed not only his $100,000, but the friendship of his beaten adversary.

STEVE RUDDOCK'S 10 COMMANDMENTS OF POKER

'Every poker player,' insists card pro Steve Ruddock, 'knows that the number one thing you must do at all times to be successful is always play your best.' But how do you know you are playing at your peak? By following what should be the '10 commandments' for any successful player, Ruddock says.

1. Thou shalt always make rational decisions

Don't let either your ego or your conscience influence your choices.

2. Thou shalt always think positively

To become a winner, you must first believe you are a winner. When others come to share this belief, they will avoid heads-up confrontations with you, and staying positive after a bad beat will prevent you from going on tilt.

3. Thou shalt only play good starting hands

If you stay tight, you'll find yourself ahead pre-flop more often than not.

4. Thou shalt be selectively aggressive

Bet and raise not just when you have the edge, but when you believe you can face down a better hand. This strategy doesn't just maximise your winnings – it minimises losses.

5. Thou shalt mix up thy play

To make money at poker, you need to be able to make people bet against your strongest hands. If you become too readable, they'll pick up the warning signs and fold.

6. Thou shalt know and play the percentages

If you know and apply the odds, you will always make the correct decision, at least from the mathematical standpoint.

7. Thou shalt always work on improving thy game

Read books. Use computer programmes. Visit online poker forums. Do whatever it takes.

8. Thou shalt learn from thy mistakes

Bad players blame bad luck for their mistakes. Good ones notice their own errors and correct them.

9. Thou shalt always pay attention

Watch your opponents and learn their play, even when you're not involved in a hand. Analyse betting patterns and try to work out what their starting hand requirements are.

10. Thou shalt be a well-rounded poker player

Don't limit yourself to hold 'em or any other form of poker. By learning other forms, you'll improve your overall play and give yourself a better chance of finding a good game.

'Breaking even one of these commandments,' Steve cautions in conclusion, 'will significantly cut into your profits, and will keep you from playing your best poker.'

POKER NICKNAMES

Nothing says 'tough guy' at the table better than a nickname. A good poker name should identify you, help you stand out from the crowd... and be true, after a fashion. Here are 15 of the best currently fleecing opponents on the world circuit:

1. Toto 'The Ripper' Leonidas
2. Barry 'The Robin Hood of Poker' Greenstein
3. Dave 'The Devilfish' Ulliott
4. Antonio 'The Magician' Esfandiari
5. Hans 'Tuna' Lund
6. Martin 'The Knife' de Knijff
7. Phil 'Unabomber' Laak
8. Mike 'The Grinder' Mizrachi
9. Men 'The Master' Nguyen
10. Jim 'The Nit' Meehan
11. Paul 'Eskimo' Clark
12. Mike 'The Mouth' Matusow
13. Howard 'Bub' Lederer
14. Phil 'The Brat' Hellmuth
15. Chris 'Jesus' Ferguson

'The Robin Hood of Poker' Greenstein, for example, got his nickname because he donates his tournament winnings to charity; 'Bub' Lederer used to be known as 'Bubba', but he lost so much weight that his friends decided to halve his nickname too; and 2000 World Series of Poker champ 'Jesus' Ferguson sports Christ-like shoulder-length hair complete with a neat moustache and beard.

20-CARD POKER

In its earliest incarnation, dating roughly to the years 1825 to 1857, poker was a game played with only 20 cards, the pack consisting solely of 10s and court cards. The earliest descriptions of the game that have survived come from the 1830s and describe a game in which the players cut the cards to determine who would deal, the winner of each pot dealing the next hand to be played. The practice of rotating the deal did not come in until the emergence of draw poker, played first with 32 cards and then a full deck of 52, in the mid 1830s. Straights and flushes were then unknown, four of a kind being the best possible hand. By 1860, an authority on card games could state that 'at the present day, what is termed "draw bluff" is played more extensively, perhaps, than the old way of playing the game', but 20-card poker continued to be a feature of New York gaming houses until just before the American Civil War.

BEWARE THE ONE-EYED MAN

The Wild West was a hotbed of poker superstitions, some of which survive, in modified form, today. Famous frontier gamblers such as Wyatt Earp and 'Wild Bill' Hickok were among the first to convince themselves that it was bad luck to count chips at the table and that failing fortunes could be revived by walking around one's chair. Perhaps the strangest Western superstition – in a dangerous time when physical disabilities were more common than they are today – was that players who sat down to poker with a one-eyed man would be permanently jinxed. In many frontier saloons, 'there's a one-eyed man in the game' was a phrase that soon came to imply that someone at the table was a cheat.

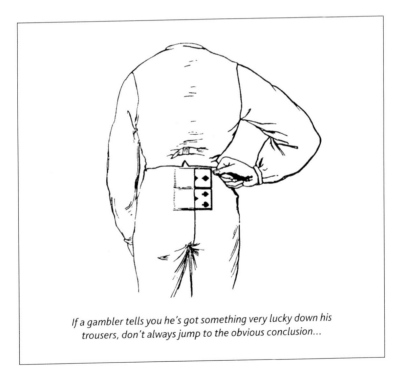

If a gambler tells you he's got something very lucky down his trousers, don't always jump to the obvious conclusion...

POKER FOOD

The Reuben Sandwich

Poker has given America one of its best-loved sandwiches, the Reuben. To the English palate it's a rather scary sounding mix of meat, cabbage, cheese and salad dressing, which is wedged between two slices of rye bread and then fried.

Although long associated with Reuben's Deli in New York, the original was invented in Omaha at the Blackstone Hotel in 1925, when local grocer Reuben Kulakofsky made sandwiches from whatever was available for guests at late-night poker games. Charles Schimmel, the hotel's owner, liked the combination so much he put it on the menu. Years later, in 1956, a waitress who'd worked at the Blackstone Hotel entered the sandwich in a national sandwich contest and won.

If you want to find out what all the fuss is about, you'll need the following to make four rather substantial sandwiches:

**Eight slices rye bread – you may want to cut the loaf lengthways
rather than down
175ml (6fl oz) thousand-island salad dressing
450g (1lb) sauerkraut, squeezed dry
Eight 30g (1oz) slices of Swiss cheese such as Emmenthal
680g (1¹/₂lb) corned beef
30g (2 tbsp) unsalted butter, melted**

Spread each slice of bread with salad dressing, using half. Assemble the ingredients as follows: rye bread, slice of cheese, a quarter of the sauerkraut drizzled with a quarter of the rest of the salad dressing, 170g (6oz) thinly sliced corned beef, another slice of cheese, then rye bread again. Brush the top with melted butter.

Heat a non-stick frying pan, flip the sandwiches and place in the pan with a heavy weight on top – a cast-iron casserole is ideal. Fry for five to 10 minutes, then brush the top side with more melted butter, flip and fry for a further five to 10 minutes until toasty and golden.

WOMEN OF POKER

Roxi Rhodes

Roxanne 'Roxi' Rhodes, one of the top female poker professionals in the United States, is a mother of five who makes a point of exploiting both her feminine wiles and the egos of her male opponents at the table.

The Granite Bay, California, professional, who made more than $100,000 playing the game in 2004, teaches poker to sold-out, women-only classes. 'We're still a novelty and a distraction,' she tells her students. 'Flirtation can be a very effective weapon.'

Like any good poker pro, the blonde and glamourous Rhodes has no compunction about taking advantage of men who underestimate her. 'I know I have an automatic advantage when a man apologises to me for taking my money,' she says.

Rhodes' husband concedes that female intuition can be a real advantage at the table. 'Their judgement is also less clouded by ego,' he adds. 'Women who think they have a bad hand are much more likely to put it down than men.'

POKER PUZZLER

Old-time poker pros gloried in exotic monikers – and many up-and-coming sharks are finding that a memorable nickname can pay dividends in their increasingly media-savvy business. It can be tricky, though, to finger a fake when you have real players with names like Dave 'The Devilfish' Ulliott around. Could you spot the ringer if you found yourself sitting down to a few hands with these players?

a) Greg 'Fossilman' Raymer
b) 'Swami' Dennis Waterman
c) Doc 'The Prince of Docness' Kegal
d) Joe 'The Elegance' Beevers
e) Zelong 'Freeman' Dong
f) Eleanor 'Madame Moustache' Dumont
g) Patrick 'Ping-Pong' Klass
h) Randy 'Dream Crusher' Jenson

Answer on page 153.

SONGS FOR GAMBLERS

'The Gambler' ....Johnny Cash
'Ace of Spades' ....Motörhead
'Cheaters Never Win'...Terry Borders
'The Card Cheat' ....The Clash
'Gamblin' Man' ....Lonnie Donegan
'Lily, Rosemary and the Jack of Hearts'...Bob Dylan
'Lottery Song' ....Harry Nilsson
'Buckin' the Dice' ....Fats Waller
'(Win, Place or Show) She's a Winner'...The Intruders
'The Cheater' ....Jimmy McCracklin
'Deal' ....Grateful Dead

THE ORIGINS OF POKER

Certain authorities say that poker, as first played in New Orleans during the 1820s, was simply a version of the ancient Persian game called 'as nas'. The Persian game was played with hands of five cards and recognised pairs, trips, four of a kind and the full house.

As nas dates to the fourteenth century and was traditionally played by four players using a deck of 20 cards divided into four suits: lions, kings, ladies and dancing girls. There was no draw; hands were bet and then shown, allowing for an element of bluff. It was not until America introduced 32-card poker that more than four players could sit down to a game.

Once established in the American South, poker developed quickly as players borrowed elements from earlier games. Features stolen from the likes of post and pair, ambigu and bouilotte include the ante, the raise before the draw, the draw itself, the freeze-out, bluffing, straights and flushes. Brag, hugely popular in England and the northern United States, lent bluffing and wild cards to poker. Brag dates to the seventeenth century and was described in Seymour's *Court Gamester* (1719) as 'the endeavour to impose on the judgement of the rest who play, and particularly on the person who chiefly offers to oppose you, by boasting or bragging of the cards in your hand'.

JUST ONE MATCH

In one $600-$1,200 game at the Mirage in Las Vegas, gambler Ted Forrest squared off against Hamid Dastmalchi, the 1992 world champion, in a non-stop, four-day bout of poker. Both men were renowned for their iron constitutions and ability to play as many as 100 hours at a stretch, but in the end it was Dastmalchi who cracked first. After he was removed from the casino in an ambulance, Forrest remarked that his opponent's condition was the result of all the bad beats he had taken. Fellow gamblers suggested it had more to do with the estimated 50 packs of cigarettes Dastmalchi had puffed his way through during the brutal session. 'And he only lit one match,' Forrest concedes when he tells the story.

SECOND DEALING

The technique of second dealing is one of the most important that any aspiring card sharp masters. Done correctly, the trick is imperceptible to even the keenest eye.

To deal the second card in a deck rather than the first, the sharper pushes both a short way forward, then slides them in opposite directions, the second card forward and the first card back. Relaxing the right hand's hold of the topmost card completely, the sharper draws off and deals the second.

Good card sharps can execute the movement in an instant, often making a tiny backwards move with their left hand as they advance the right, which completely masks the change.

WHEN IS A THIEF NOT A THIEF?

'I wasn't actually stealing the money, just using it temporarily.' This was the unusual explanation given by Portland State University library employee Mary Joan Byrd, 61, when she was prosecuted in 1997 for taking more than $200,000 from the school's copy machines. Charged with stealing from the State of Oregon, Byrd explained that she took the money, conveniently in small change, in order to play video poker games licensed by the state, and since she'd never won anything, the state still had all its money.

POKER FOOD

Premier Poker Eating

You're sitting around playing a few hands, and everyone's getting peckish. You want something to eat, but nothing too distracting – something you can eat while playing without making a mess. Sandwiches seem the obvious choice, but offering a piece of plastic ham slapped between two slices of bread somehow doesn't seem hospitable. Here's the secret of hassle-free poker eating. Have to hand:

A couple of flat, whole focaccia loaves
Olive oil
A selection of artichokes, mushrooms, peppers and
sun-dried tomatoes, all bottled in oil
Three or four round buffalo-mozzarella cheeses
Some ready-sliced Swiss cheese or cheddar
Some sliced ham – Parma if you're feeling flush

Cut your loaves in half, sprinkle inside with olive oil and bang into the oven (on about 200°C) on a baking sheet to crisp – it doesn't matter if you've only just put the oven on. While they're toasting, get a big bowl and empty in your drained (but still oily) veg. Anything that's too big, cut into bite-sized pieces. Cut the mozzarella into cubes and the other cheese and ham into strips. Mix so it's all coated with the oil from the veg.

Take the half-loaves out of the oven, dump on your filling mix, sandwich together and put a heavy weight (such as a casserole lid) on top, then stick back in the now-hot oven for 10 to 15 minutes to heat up. The cheese will melt and stick together all the other ingredients and the bread will crisp up so it doesn't crumble when you bite into it. There's no salad dressing or mayo to drip, nothing to slide out... et voila – the perfect poker sarnie.

CARD SHARP

Let's face it, gambling is a very romantic activity. We all daydream about people doing something we are a little bit afraid to do, and we make heroes out of those who pull it off.
Jack Binion, casino executive

POKER HANDS RANKED

Royal flush
Ten, J, Q, K, A in the same suit. If two players have royal flushes, they tie.

Straight flush
Any five cards in sequence, in the same suit. If two players have straight flushes, the one with the highest-ranking card in it wins.

Four of a kind
Four cards of the same denomination plus a 'kicker'. If two players have four of a kind, the player with the highest-ranking four of a kind wins.

Full house
Three cards of the same denomination plus a pair. If two players have a full house, the player with the highest-ranking three of a kind wins.

Flush
Any five non-consecutive cards in the same suit. If two players have a flush, the player with the highest-ranking card wins.

Straight
Any five cards in numerical sequence, irrespective of suit. If two players have a straight, the player with the highest-ranking card wins.

Three of a kind
Three cards of the same denomination. If two players have three of a kind, the player with the highest-ranking three of a kind wins.

Two pair
Two cards of the same denomination twice. If two players have two pairs, the highest pair wins. If they both have the same high pair the highest second pair wins. If they both have identical pairs, the highest kicker card making up the hand wins.

Pair
Two cards of the same denomination. If two players have a pair, the highest pair wins.

High card
If none of the hands above are completed, the highest card in any hand wins.

POKER IN PROSE

They give me a great big room at the hotel in Pittsburgh; so the fellers picked it out for the poker game. We was playin' along about ten o'clock one night when in come Elliott – the earliest he'd showed up since we'd been roomin' together. They was only five of us playin' and Tom ast him to sit in.

'I'm busted,' he says.

'Can you play poker?' I ast him.

'They's nothin' I can't do!' he says. 'Slip me a couple o' bucks and I'll show you.'

So I slipped him a couple o' bucks and honestly hoped he'd win, because I knowed he never had no dough. Well, Tom dealt him a hand and he picks it up and says:

'I only got five cards.'

'How many do you want?' I says.

'Oh,' he says, 'if that's all I get I'll try to make 'em do.'

The pot was cracked and raised, and he stood the raise. I says to myself: 'There goes my two bucks!' But no – he comes out with three queens and won the dough. It was only about seven bucks; but you'd of thought it was a million to see him grab it. He laughed like a kid.

'Guess I can't play this game!' he says; and he had me fooled for a minute – I thought he must of been kiddin' when he complained of only havin' five cards.

He copped another pot right afterward and was sittin' there with about eleven bucks in front of him when Jim opens a roodle pot for a buck. I stays and so does Elliott. Him and Jim both drawed one card and I took three.[...]

'How much can I bet?' says the bug.

'You can raise Jim a buck if you want to,' I says.

So he bets two dollars. Jim comes back at him. He comes right back at Jim. Jim raises him again and he tilts Jim right back. Well, when he'd boosted Jim with the last buck he had, Jim says:

'I'm ready to call. I guess you got me beat. What have you got?'

'I know what I've got, all right,' says Elliott. 'I've got a straight.' And he throws his hand down. Sure enough, it was a straight, eight high. Jim pretty near fainted and so did I.

The bug had started pullin' in the dough when Jim stops him.

'Here! Wait a minute!' says Jim. 'I thought you had somethin'. I filled up.' Then Jim lays down his nine full.

'You beat me, I guess,' says Elliott, and he looked like he'd lost his last friend.

'Beat you?' says Jim. 'Of course I beat you! What did you think I had?'

'Well,' says the bug, 'I thought you might have a small flush or somethin'.'

When I regained consciousness he was beggin' for two more bucks.

Ring W Lardner, *Round Up* (1929)

INTERNATIONAL POKER FEDERATION TOP RANKED PLAYERS 2005

Ranking	Name	Nationality
1.	Maciel Gracz	United States
2.	Raja Kattamuri	United States
3.	Thuan 'Scotty' Nguyen	United States
4.	Erik Seidel	United States
5.	Chris 'Jesus' Ferguson	United States
6.	John Phan	United States
7.	John Stolzmann	United States
8.	Paul Maxfield	England
9.	Allen Cunningham	United States
10.	Joe Hachem	Australia

POKER MILLIONAIRES

The World Series of Poker keeps a record of every player who's won more than a million dollars, whether it's in a single tournament or over a lifetime. Given the huge prizes these days for winning major tournaments and the fact that players can win money even if they come in at 25th (and in some cases lower), some of the younger players are already multimillionaires while money amassed by older players struggles to reach seven figures.

Mickey Appelman	Layne Flack	Tom McEvoy
Jim Bechtel	Noel Furlong	Chris Moneymaker
John Bonetti	Julian Gardner	Carlos Mortenson
Humberto Brenes	Russ Hamilton	Men 'The Master' Nguyen
Doyle Brunson	Dan Harrington	Scotty Nguyen
Brent Carter	Jay Heimowitz	Huck Seed
Johnny Chan	Phil Hellmuth	Erik Seidel
David Chiu	Chris Ferguson	Dewey Tomko
TJ Cloutier	Berry Johnston	Stuey Ungar
Hamid Dastmalchi	Mel Judah	Robert Varkonyi
Brad Daugherty	Jack Keller	
Sam Farha	Mansour Matloubi	

POKER WIT & WISDOM

POKER PUZZLER

What's the upwardly mobile name given to the highest-value chips being played in a card room?

a) Top Table
b) Big Ticket
c) High Society
d) Upper Crust

Answer on page 153.

HALL OF FAME

Being inducted into Binion's Poker Hall of Fame is the poker equivalent of having a star in the pavement in Hollywood – only for the legends. Since Binion's Horseshoe casino started the tradition in 1979, only 22 players have been inducted. They began by inducting seven legendary players in the first year, adding to them only when the quality of performance warranted it. Here's that first lucky seven...

Johnny Moss
The first World Series of Poker winner, who went on to win it twice more, a feat only equalled by Stuey Ungar.

Red Winn
Winn is remembered as a player who could play every type of poker, no matter what the regional variation, and quickly work out how to win.

Nick 'The Greek' Dandalos
Dandalos was narrowly beaten by Johnny Moss in a marathon Las Vegas game in 1949, and over his lifetime won (and lost) an estimated $50m.

James Butler 'Wild Bill' Hickok
Hickok's legendary life and death was recorded in thousands of folk-tales, songs and pulp novels. A semi-professional gambler, he was also a sheriff, cavalryman and Union spy during the Civil War.

Felton 'Corky' McCorquodale
A professional gambler, McCorquodale introduced Texas hold 'em to Las Vegas back in 1963 and changed the path of poker playing forever.

Sid Wyman
Wyman was famous both as a player and a dealer, and owned shares in several legendary Vegas casinos during the 1950s, 1960s and 1970s.

Edmond Hoyle
Hoyle is perhaps a surprise entry, given that he lived in eighteenth-century London before poker was even developed. He earned part of his living by teaching card games, particularly whist, and wrote one of the seminal books on the subject, *A Short Treatise on the Game of Whist*, which defined the different games played in London society at the time.

A BAD BEAT

William C Ralston, president of the Bank of California in the latter half of the nineteenth century, was among the finest poker players of his day. One of his most difficult opponents was William Sharon, the renowned San Francisco gambler, who in the early 1870s, took one of the baddest beats in poker history while the men were playing head-to-head. The game was jackpots (p147), and there was already $150,000 in the middle of the table when Sharon raised his friend a further $50,000. Ralston countered with a $150,000 raise, taking the pot to an unprecedented $350,000 and forcing Sharon to fold. The gambler had already shuffled his cards back into the deck when Ralston showed his hand, displaying a pair of tens. Sharon maintained a dignified silence, and it was only after Ralston drowned on the day after his bank failed in 1875 that the beaten man revealed the cards he had held during that memorable hand: a pair of jacks.

WEIGHTY MATTERS

The greatest poker players are invariably gamblers at heart, not business people – and they regularly prove the point by losing money at craps, betting heavily on sports and indulging in eccentric wagers. One of the maddest bets began when 6ft 6in pro Huck Seed, a wiry 180lb, made a New Year's resolution to start weight training to bulk up, while Howard Lederer, at over 300lb, made one to diet. Fellow gambler Mike Svobodny bet the two men $50,000 each that they could not cross over weights at some point during the year. Seed, training regularly, actually lost 4lb and Lederer struggled so badly to lose weight that he eventually booked himself in for gastric bypass surgery. The two men never did meet in the middle and ended up paying out.

INDUCTED BECAUSE HE GOT INDICTED

Freddy 'Sarge' Ferris, who was inducted into the Poker Hall of Fame in 1989, had gained renown six years earlier thanks to an unusual brush with the law. Sarge was taking part in a high-stakes side game during the World Series of Poker when a team of IRS inspectors swooped on his table looking to recover unpaid taxes. When Ferris was unable to pay his debt in cash, the taxmen seized $46,000 worth of chips from the stack in front of him, took them to the desk and cashed them in.

RORY MONAHAN'S ONLINE MISTAKES

With so many players cutting their teeth online, here are Rory Monahan's thoughts on what the novice player needs to look out for:

1. Stay focused Pay attention to detail and don't get distracted by what's going on at home. Rory advises turning off the TV, your phone and anything else that could interrupt you while at play.

2. Don't use auto-play functions They may speed up the game, but they cost you too many chips and 'tell' your opponents what you're up to by making your play predictable.

3. Don't chat while playing Like any communication at a poker table, it helps other players. 'Don't waste your energy taunting or talking to other players,' advises Rory. 'This will give players a look into your personality and therefore your true playing style.'

4. Don't make enemies Because no one's actually going to punch you in the face, most people find it easier to get aggressive online than in person. You're there to play poker, not have a fight.

5. Never show your cards unless you have to. It only gives people information about how and when you bluff.

6. Don't rely too much on odds If the improbable never happened, bees would be ground insects. In poker you're always playing the other player as much as the cards.

7. Stick to your limits If you play at a table when you cannot afford to lose all your money, you will play too conservatively and will quickly go broke. Start with too little money and you can be bullied out of a game or be tempted to spend next month's housekeeping money in order to stay in.

CARD SHARP

There are few things that are so unpardonably neglected in our country as poker. The upper class knows very little about it. Now and then you find ambassadors who have sort of a general knowledge of the game, but the ignorance of the people is fearful. Why, I have known clergymen, good men, kind-hearted, liberal, sincere and all that, who did not know the meaning of a flush. It is enough to make one ashamed of one's species.
Mark Twain, from *A Bibliography of Mark Twain*, edited by Merle Johnson

DON'T TELL

When Andy Beal, a multimillionaire banker, began playing heads-up no-limit hold 'em against a dozen top pros in 2001 – the biggest game of poker ever played – he realised that his opponents were reading him better than he could read them. With upwards of $10m changing hands in the course of a session, his tells were costing him a fortune. Here are the five steps Beal took to improve his game and make himself unreadable.

1. Conceal the eyes
Great poker players can tell everything about an opponent's hands by looking into their eyes. Beal purchased numerous pairs of sunglasses and experimented until he found a comfortable pair that also completely shielded him.

2. Block out all noise
Beal guessed some opponents were analysing tiny changes in his speech pattern. Purchasing earplugs and an MP3 player to block out all distractions, he played in total silence.

3. Randomise decision making
After taking several huge beats at Andy's hands, players such as Ted Forrest were judging the strength of his hand by timing his decisions. Beal took a crucial second or two more to think about moderate hands and that was enough to give the pros an edge. When he spotted this weakness, Andy built a tiny battery-operated motor that he placed in his sock which buzzed every eight seconds. Beal trained himself to make a decision – but only execute it the next time the motor buzzed.

4. Get yourself an edge
Beal saw that the pros based their decisions as much on reading character as on their cards. Beal wrote himself a computer program that analysed millions of hands to calculate factors that even the greatest players never really considered – things such as: 'What is the lowest high card you could have in your hand and expect to win more than half the time regardless of the second card?'*

5. Out-think your opponent
Andy created an equation that would help him refine the accuracy of decisions such as when to check. If an opponent folded four times in 10, he'd raise 40% of the time. He used a watch with only a second hand as a sort of random number generator to determine if his current hand should fall into that 40%.

* A king. Beal's program revealed that K-2 offsuit won between 52.6% and 53.2% of the time, while Q-2 offsuit won at most 49.4% of hands.

THE TRAIN TAKEDOWN

Although the Hollywood picture of a Wild West gambler is a tall, saturnine man with piercing eyes, dressed all in black, sipping bourbon in the saloon of a dusty frontier town, professional gamblers of the time came in all shapes and sizes, and practised all sorts of arts to make a living. The two skills that united the successful were a facility with knife and pistol, and a willingness to use them if things got sticky, as they so often did.

When *Harper's Magazine* journalist George Jean Nathan interviewed a lifelong professional gambler, the portrait he painted was of a grey-haired, benign-looking man who remarked that much of his income came from working the trains. The gambler explained that he and two partners would board a long-distance train, often returning to the same train again and again over a period of months. They would pretend they didn't know each other and start a game of poker among themselves, then casually invite a rich-looking 'sucker' to join them. Shortly thereafter one would accuse their mark of cheating and another would grab him and 'find' a concealed card about his person, an easy ruse for the light-fingered professional. Threatening to expose him as a cheat, the gang would take their victim's money. The idea of losing their reputation seemed to have a powerful effect on most people, but sometimes the card sharps would simply hold up the rest of the players in the game. In one six-month period working a Denver train, the interviewee estimated he and his partner had netted $30,000, including $5,000 from one hold-up alone.

TRUMAN'S BUCK

Many people think President Truman coined the phrase 'The buck stops here', but in fact it was a line inspired by poker. Truman had a sign on his desk, given to him by a US Marshal from Missouri, to which he often referred. The Marshal, in turn had seen a similar sign at the Federal Reformatory at El Reno, Oklahoma, and thought it would be a good motto for a President.

It derives from the common phrase 'To pass the buck', which some authorities think refers to the marker, originally a buckhorn-handled knife and then a disc made from buckhorn, used in a game of poker. Thus a player who didn't want to deal had to pass the buck to someone else.

BEFORE POKER THERE WAS FARO

Although it first came to prominence along the Mississippi during the 1830s, poker did not become America's favourite card game until the first years of the twentieth century. Before that time, another, now-forgotten, game held sway throughout America and Europe. This was faro – named for the portrait of an Egyptian monarch that once appeared on French card decks – which owed its popularity to the fact that, of all games played by gamblers, it offered the least advantage to the bank; the margin in the house's favour was generally reckoned to be little more than 1.5%. 'An almost conclusive argument,' one gambler observed in 1900, 'for the theory that the percentage at honest faro is virtually non-existent is the fact that the canny management of Monte Carlo has never permitted the game to be played at that celebrated resort.'

Gamblers playing faro wagered not against each other but against the house, betting on the order of cards drawn from a dealing case. The first card out of the box was regarded as dead. Thereafter, cards were pulled out two at a time, the first in each pair being the bank's and the second, the player's. Thus if a gambler bet on, say, the dealing of a four, and a four was drawn on the bank's turn, the gambler lost. If the card emerged on the player's turn, the player won. If two fours were drawn together, bets were split. Success in faro depended on the ability to count cards while keeping track of an often-complex pattern of bets placed on a colourfully marked board. The game's influence, like that of poker, can be gauged from the number of faro terms that found their way into everyday English. Players tracked the cards that had been dealt by 'keeping tabs', and 'broke even' when they bet a card to win and lose an equal number of times; others preferred 'stringing along', a method for betting on 21 different groups of cards simultaneously.

POKER PUZZLER

Which woman has made it furthest in the WSOP main event?

a) Jennifer Harman
b) Barbara Enright
c) Annie Duke
d) Jennifer Tilly

Answer on page 153.

CARD SHARP

I've lost money so fast in these clubs it's left me reeling. I've read every poker book ever written, but the only way to get better at the game is to go out and play with people who are really good. The problem is, you stand to lose a lot of money doing it.
Matt Damon, actor

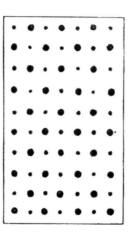

If you can pick out which of the dots on this card-marking grid is the significant one, we'll be damned.

FIVE ROUNDS A DAY

Poker player Huck Seed – something of a mean golfer, too – once won a huge cash bet that he could not play four rounds of golf at under 96 in a single day, without a cart, using only three clubs. Teeing off at the height of the Nevada summer, he won the bet despite having to play five times in all – the first time round he carded 96 exactly.

AMARILLO SLIM'S RULES OF ROAD GAMBLING

Amarillo Slim cut his poker-playing teeth travelling around the South, playing cards and hustling pool wherever he could find a game, in the days before organised tournaments, casino safes and guaranteed jackpots. Here are his simple rules for playing poker on the hoof.

1. Find the game
2. Beat the game
3. Not get arrested
4. Not get robbed

ALL-TIME BIGGEST MONEY WINNERS

Some people play for a lifetime to amass their total, others win it all in a single game, like WSOP champion 2002 Robert Varkonyi, or the 2003 winner, the appropriately named Chris Moneymaker.

Phil Hellmuth	$3,526,750	Erik Seidel	$2,362,621
Johnny Chan	$3,477,634	Stuey Ungar	$2,018,478
TJ Cloutier	$2,992,841	Robert Varkonyi	$2,000,000
Chris Ferguson	$2,514,572	Dan Harrington	$1,975,858
Chris Moneymaker	$2,500,000	Huck Seed	$1,929,894

THE MOST FAMOUS DECK OF CARDS EVER PRINTED

When Brigadier General Vincent Brooks of the US Army called a press conference on 11 April 2003, the gathered journalists had no idea they were about to be shown a deck of cards. The Central Command Deputy Director of Operations proceeded to display a pack of cards, each card printed with an identification photo (if available) and details of the US's most wanted Iraqis.

Thousands of packs were originally printed for military personnel, in the hope that they would either play cards with them and thus become familiar with the faces of the most wanted war criminals, or carry them around as a quick reference when on patrol, should they come across someone who looked familiar. The packs quickly became collectors' items, and were hugely in demand in America and Europe.

POKER IN PROSE

Travelling cross-country by train on his way to make his famous 'Iron Curtain' speech in 1946, Winston Churchill challenges Harry S Truman and his aides to a little poker.

A few minutes later, with dinner completed, Churchill excused himself for a moment. The moment he had left, the President turned to us, and, in total seriousness, said, 'Men, we have an important task ahead of us. This man is cagey, he loves cards, and is probably an excellent player. The reputation of American poker is at stake, and I expect every man to do his duty.'

Churchill returned to the dining room dressed in his famous Second World War zippered blue siren suit, which I thought looked a bit like a bunny suit. The steward put a green baize cover over the dining room table and six of us sat down for the most memorable poker game in which I ever played. The truth emerged quickly: however enthusiastic and proud of his poker skills, Churchill was not very good at the game. I learned later that, when playing in his own card games in England, he was excellent. But in poker, with its bluffs and values of deception, he was, so to speak, a lamb among wolves.

After about an hour, Churchill excused himself briefly. The moment the door closed President Truman turned to us, with a grave expression. 'Now look here, men – you are not treating our guest very well.' He then looked at Churchill's dwindling stack of chips. 'I fear that he may already have lost close to $300.'

Harry Vaughan looked at his friend of thirty years and laughed. 'But, Boss, this guy's a pigeon! If you want us to play our best poker for the nation's honour, we'll have this guy's pants before the evening is over. Now, you just tell us what you want. You want us to play customer poker, okay, we can carry him along all evening. If you want us to give it our best, we'll have his underwear.'

President Truman smiled. 'I don't want him to think we are pushovers, but at the same time, let's not treat him badly.'

Those were our ground rules for the rest of the trip. Finally, however, when the evening was drawing to a close, we moved in a little on our guest. When the dust had settled and we tallied up, Churchill has lost about $250. He had enjoyed himself thoroughly, but he had dropped just enough money so that he could not go back to London and, as Vaughan put it, 'brag to his Limey friends that he had beaten the Americans at poker.'

Clark Clifford, *Counsel to the President* (1991)

71

CHRIS FERGUSON'S GOLDEN RULES OF HOLD 'EM

1. PUMP IT or DUMP IT!

Never limp into a hand, advises former World Series of Poker champion Chris 'Jesus' Ferguson. And never, ever call as the first player to enter a pot before the flop. 'Either pump up the pot with a raise, or dump your cards in the muck,' Chris says. 'If your hand isn't strong enough for a raise, it's too weak for a call. This tactic makes it more difficult for your opponents to read your hand, and it makes it impossible for the big blind to ever see a flop for free when you're in the hand.'

2. Never bet medium-strength hands

Poker players bet their best hands, hoping to get called. And they often bet their worst hands, too, as a bluff, hoping for the better hands to fold. But, 'Jesus' warns, 'an average hand doesn't work either way. You can't get better hands to fold and your chance of getting weaker hands to call is too slim to justify a bet. Just check it down and hope your hand is good enough to drag in the chips.'

3. Mix up your play

It's all too easy to give away your hand playing straightforward poker. 'Mix it up a little,' Ferguson says. 'Early in the hand, play your pocket rockets like a small pair once in a while. And play that 5d-6d like it's K-K. Keep them guessing, but don't overdo it or an attentive opponent will catch on, this play will lose its effectiveness and you will lose your chips.'

From Chris Ferguson's official website.

HALL OF FAME

After inducting seven members in its inaugural year, the Poker Hall of Fame stuck with one a year, choosing from old-school road gamblers, Vegas fixtures and masters of different poker variations.

1980 – T 'Blondie' Forbes

Remembered as a veteran road gambler who followed the big games all over Texas and adjacent states.

1981 – Bill Boyd

Five-card stud was Boyd's game, and he won the world championships five years in a row from 1970 to 1974, as well as managing the card room at the Golden Nugget casino from 1946 to 1982.

1982 – Tom Abdo

Lifelong gambler and poker aficionado. When Abdo had a heart attack while playing poker, his last words were to count his chips and save his seat.

WILD BILL'S FULL HOUSE

One of the most celebrated Wild West poker tales concerns 'Wild Bill' Hickok's encounters with a sharp poker player by the name of McDonald. McDonald beat Hickok on several occasions, and the gunman's friends warned him that he was being cheated. Next time the two men sat down to play a no-limit head-to-head, Bill began to bet heavily on what seemed to be an excellent hand. McDonald raised him every time and, at the showdown, turned over three jacks.

'I have a full house, aces and sixes,' Hickok replied.

'Aces full on sixes wins,' conceded McDonald, but when he leaned forward to check Hickok's hand, he found only two aces and one six.

'Now, hold on,' the gambler snapped, but as he did so, Hickok pulled his six-shooter with his right hand. 'Here's my other six,' he snarled, drawing a bowie knife from its sheath with his left. 'And here's my one spot.'

McDonald exhaled sharply. 'That hand is good,' he said. 'You take the pot.'

POKER FOOD

Cocktails

It may not be wise to drink and gamble, but for many they're pleasures that go hand in hand. So it's not surprising that bar tenders have invented several cocktails in honour of the game including:

The Poker Cocktail

Fill a tall glass with ice cubes. Pour over 3 measures of tequila and 1 measure of cointreau or other orange liqueur. Fill up with pineapple juice. Stir, add a wedge of lime, and enjoy.

The Poker

The Poker, on the other hand, is clearly intended for the more serious liver-picklers out there. Mix equal measures of white or golden run and dry vermouth. Stir in a jug with plenty of ice, then strain into a classic, chilled cocktail glass and serve.

POKER'S BIGGEST EVER RAISE

John Dougherty, although often overlooked today, was probably the most famous gambler in Tombstone during its Wild West heyday. And that was no mean feat, as the town was packed with card sharps of all kinds. Like most professional gamblers of his day, Dougherty carried a revolver, but unlike most of them, he wasn't a particularly good shot or at all inclined to draw it. Instead of prowess with a gun, Dougherty was famous for two things: the huge stakes he was willing to play for, and the smallness of his feet, something he was extremely proud of.

Dougherty was known to carry a bankroll of around $100,000, and only played no-limit games for high stakes – he refused to play if the other players didn't display enough wealth for his liking. In 1889, Dougherty agreed to play Ike Johnson, a cattle baron from Colorado, for the poker championship of the West.

The two met in Santa Fe, and a hundred prominent citizens, including L Bradford Price, the Governor of New Mexico, watched as witnesses. The betting began heavily as both men drew good hands at the start. After only a few minutes the pot stood at $100,000.

Jackson rapidly began to run out of cash, so he wrote out a deed to his ranch and 10,000 head of cattle, valued at a further $100,000, and raised by the full amount.

This left Dougherty short himself, unable to call or raise. He took up the pen Johnson had used and wrote out a deed himself, handed it to the Governor and drew his gun. According to Herbert Asbury in *Sucker's Progress: An Informal History of Gambling in America from the Colonies to Canfield* (New York: Dodd, Mead & Co., 1938), he then said:

'Now, Governor, you sign this or I will kill you. I like you and would fight for you, but I love my reputation as a poker player better than I do you or any-thing else.'

Hastily Governor Price complied, without reading the document. Dougherty promptly threw it on the table and announced that he was raising Johnson the Territory of New Mexico.

'All right,' an outraged Johnson replied, 'take the pot. But it's a damned good thing for you that the Governor of Texas isn't here!'

CARD SHARP

A man who can play delightfully on a guitar and keep a knife in his boot would make an excellent poker player.
WJ Florence, *Handbook on Poker* (1891)

AL ALVAREZ – THE POKER POET

Few people can claim to have parallel careers as a poker player and a poet, but Al Alvarez has combined a lifelong love of the game with his writing career, producing volumes of poetry, novels and several excellent non-fiction books on topics as diverse as suicide, North Sea oil, divorce, mountaineering and of course the game he adores (*The Biggest Game In Town* and *Poker: Bets, Bluffs and Bad Beats*). Many professionals name *The Biggest Game In Town* as their favourite book about poker.

A friend of Ted Hughes and Sylvia Path, the Oxford-educated Alvarez was poetry critic for *The Observer* for 10 years and moves effortlessly between the worlds of letters and the card table – although later critics may wonder whether the two-decade hiatus in publishing poetry, from 1978 to 2002, was due to non-fiction projects or his striving to improve his poker face.

He normally plays in clubs, although he misses being able to smoke his pipe there, and has said that he'd like to go out at the poker table. 'It's going to finish when I fold my hand and go up to the big poker game in the sky.'

RAGS – THE WORST HAND TO WIN THE WORLD SERIES

The worst hand ever to win the World Series of Poker was the J♣ 6♥ dealt to Jim Bechtel at the climax of the 1993 event's final head-to-head. Bechtel's opponent, Glen Cozen, received an even more unpromising 7♠ 4♦, but with a dwindling pile of chips in front of him, blinds of $5,000 to $10,000, and a $2,000 ante, he had little room for manoeuvre – as Bechtel knew full well. Cozen went all in, Bechtel called, and with a flop of 10♦ 8♠ 3♣ helping neither man, everything rested on the turn and the river. 9-6, 5-6 or any 7 or 4 would have been enough to win the pot for Cozen, but the cards came up 2♣ 5♦. Bechtel had won a cool $1m with rags, jack high.

HALL OF FAME

During the early years of the Poker Hall of Fame they added a new name every year, recognising figures from the early history of the game as well as current greats.

1983 – Joe Bernstein
Legendary road gambler during the 1920s and 1930s who in later life gambled at the Horseshoe and was recognised by his fancy clothes.

1984 – Murph Harrold
One of the best deuce-to-seven draw or Kansas City lowball players of all time.

1985 – Red Hodges
The king of seven-card stud, regarded as one of the best players of that particular variant who ever lived.

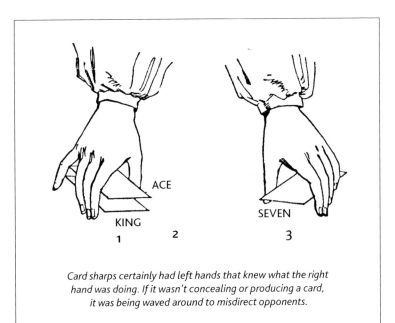

Card sharps certainly had left hands that knew what the right hand was doing. If it wasn't concealing or producing a card, it was being waved around to misdirect opponents.

WOMEN OF POKER

Mini Minnie

The most famous poker dealer of the nineteenth century was a four-foot nothing firebrand known as Minnie the Gambler, a renowned card sharp and bottom dealer capable of expertly manipulating any pack of cards. Minnie was the girlfriend of Colorado Charley Utter, 'Wild Bill' Hickok's one-time gambling partner, and dealt stud poker for him in El Paso until 1904. The Wild West was getting a little tame by then, and, in search of more excitement, the couple packed up and organised a medicine show, which they toured through Mexico and South America until Charley's death. Minnie must have been a very canny dealer, though, for she was by then wealthy enough to retire to Southern California with a comfortable fortune.

TELL IT AS IT IS

Mike Caro, the self-proclaimed 'Mad Genius of Poker', is famous for his study of tells – giveaway, subconscious actions that can reveal almost everything about the strength of an opponent's hand. In *Caro's Book of Poker Tells*, Mike distils his wisdom into a collection of nearly 60 key tells, ranking them by category and discussing their meaning.

Among the most critical tells is Caro's discovery that the way in which players stack their chips is a key indicator of their likely style of play. Those who arrange their chips in neat piles, perhaps even lining up markings on the sides, are likely to play conservatively. Those who sit with ragged piles in front of them are much more likely to be undisciplined, sloppy players.

The value of this tell, Caro adds, is enhanced because chip stacking is an activity undertaken between hands, when players are more likely to be unguarded. During play, players will often consciously alter their behaviour in an attempt to bluff.

CARD SHARP

Morals are an acquirement – like music, like a foreign language, like piety, poker, paralysis – no man is born with them.
Mark Twain, US novelist, journalist, river pilot

POKER PUZZLER

In poker parlance, which of the following hands is known as a Motown?

a) 3,3,3,Q,Q

b) J,J,5,5,A

c) A,2,3,4,5

d) 5,5,3,3,Q

Answer on page 153.

POKER SLANG

Over the years, many common starting hands have acquired nicknames. Experienced players delight in baffling newcomers with poker slang, and can often scent a pigeon from their unfamiliarity with the familiar terms – so it's well worth mastering even the more obscure ones.

99	German virgin	**22**	Ducks
88	Snowmen; Doggie balls	**T5**	Five and dime
77	Sunset strip	**T4**	Good buddy
66	Route 66	**69**	Big lick
55	Speed limit	**57**	Heinz
44	Magnum	**38**	Raquel Welch
33	Crabs		

T4, 'Good buddy', has its origins in old CB radio slang, as anyone who's seen a *Smokey and the Bandit* movie will know. We'll leave the meaning of 'Big Lick' and 'Raquel Welch' to your imagination.

EYE WATERING

Proof – if any were required – that poker pros lose all touch with reality comes from Chip Reese's water bill. At a time when $50 was normal for a quarter's supply, the Vegas legend once paid a $2,000 demand without querying it, and was surprised to receive a hefty refund after the local water board discovered a major rupture in the pipes leading to his house.

POKER IN PROSE

A young man finds his girlfriend's no pushover when he plays her at poker.

'Hoh!' exclaimed Condy; 'what do YOU know of poker? I think we had best play old sledge or cassino.'

Blix had dealt a hand and partitioned the chips.

'Straights and flushes BEFORE the draw,' she announced calmly.

Condy started and stared; then, looking at her askance, picked up his hand.

'It's up to you.'

'I'll make it five to play.'

'Five? Very well. How many cards?'

'Three.'

'I'll take two.'

'Bet you five more.'

Blix looked at her hand. Then, without trace of expression in her voice or face, said:

'There's your five, and I'll raise you five.'

'Five better.'

'And five better than that.'

'Call you.'

'Full house. Aces on tens,' said Blix, throwing down her cards.

'Heavens! they're good as gold,' muttered Condy as Blix gathered in the chips.

An hour later she had won all the chips but five.

'Now we'll stop and get to fishing again; don't you want to?'

He agreed, and she counted the chips.

'Condy, you owe me seven dollars and a half,' she announced.

Condy began to smile. 'Well,' he said jocosely, 'I'll send you around a check to-morrow.'

But at this Blix was cross upon the instant. 'You wouldn't do that – wouldn't talk that way with one of your friends at the club!' she exclaimed; 'and it's not right to do it with me. Condy, give me seven dollars and a half. When you play cards with me it's just as though it were with another man. I would have paid you if you had won.'

'But I haven't got more than nine dollars. Who'll pay for the supper to-night at Luna's, and our railroad fare going home?'

'I'll pay.'

'But I – I can't afford to lose money this way.'

'Shouldn't have played, then. I took the same chances as you. Condy, I want my money.'

'You – you – why you've regularly flimflammed me.'

Frank Norris, *Blix* (1900)

79

POKER TALK

Terms from gambling have entered the English language and are now familiar to most English speakers. Some, however, remain fairly obscure. When was the last time you heard someone say 'from soda to hock', meaning from start to finish? The soda was the first card dealt from a faro box, and invalid, and the hock was the last, also invalid. Obscure phrases aside, without poker we'd have none of the following:

Cashed in his chips • Up the ante
On a roll • Dead man's hand
Read 'em and weep • Go all in
Poker face • The buck stops here
Hit me • Taken to the cleaners
Lose your shirt • The smart money's on...
Put up or shut up

LARRY FLYNT'S POKER CHALLENGE CUP

Despite being confined to a wheelchair, *Hustler Magazine* empire founder Larry Flynt manages to be a larger-than-life character in the world of poker. A skilled player of seven-card stud who has never been afraid to drop a lot of money to play with the best professionals and learn from them, Flynt created the Hustler Casino in Gardena, California, 20 minutes from Redondo Beach, which became known for high-stakes games and sexy women in not very much clothing.

Nowadays it hosts steady tournaments like the Grand Slam of Poker and the Ladies Classic – and yes, the ladies do get attended by greased up body-builders in small pants, just to be fair. Such events allow a lot of players to buy in to large tournaments at reasonable rates, but initially the casino had a reputation as a place for high flyers only. To publicise its new policy and many low-limit games, in 2003 Flynt created the Larry Flynt Poker Challenge Cup.

The 14-day, seven-card stud championship offered $1m to the winner (the biggest prize for seven-card stud), and was eventually claimed by Barry 'the Robin Hood of Poker' Greenstein, who promptly gave the money to charity. One suspects that the chance to gather the greatest seven-card stud players in the world in one room was excellent value for money as far as Flynt was concerned.

CARDS ON FILM

10 films that sound like they're the nuts!

1. *Casino* (1995) – although the casino in the movie is called The Tangiers, most of the events are based on the history of The Stardust, and Scorsese uses the song 'Stardust' three times during the film.

2. *Casino Royale* (1967) – the very first James Bond novel, originally intended as a spoof, filmed with David Niven as the ageing spy.

3. *Cleopatra Jones And The Casino of Gold* (1975) – Cleopatra Jones was an attempt to create a black Modesty Blaise during the blaxploitation frenzy.

4. *Gran Casino* (1947) – directed by Surrealist visionary Luis Brunel.

5. *4 Dogs Playing Poker* (2000) – displays a reference to the popular kitsch paintings.

6. Poker Alice – Liz Taylor and George Hamilton in a very sanitised version of Alice Ivers' career

7. *Poker at Dawson City* (1889) – this is probably the oldest film to feature poker.

8. The Gambler, the Nun and the Radio (1960) – the title is definitely the most outstanding thing about this film.

9. *Cards, Cads, Guns, Gore and Death* (1969) – early directorial effort from Ron Howard.

10. *The Cards Never Lie* (1915) – director Harry Myers appeared in 209 films and directed 39 more.

THE DRUGS DO WORK

Apart from some keen cancer-stick lovers, poker isn't a game much associated with drugs these days. But sometimes players are decidedly under the influence. Phil Hellmuth Jr tells of a time when he asked his doctor wife to prescribe some strong sleeping pills so he could get to sleep on the night before the main event at the World Poker Challenge in Reno, in 2000. When he woke up the pills were still in action, making him decidedly casual in his approach to the game. 'I was out of control at the poker table as far as my hand selection was concerned, and I was acting as though I didn't have a care in the world,' he later wrote.

After raising 12 pots in a row and bluffing wildly when anyone called him, people began to catch on when he began singing the 'Zoom zoom zoom' theme to the Mazda car adverts. However it seemed to work in Hellmuth's favour as tablemate John Bonetti told him: 'You're putting the fear of God into these people today.'

BENJAMIN 'BUGSY' SIEGEL

Bugsy Siegel is renowned, not just for his links with organised crime, but as the man who put Vegas on the map as a Mecca for gambling, just after the Second World War. This was actually towards the end of a bloody career – the last two years of his life were spent moving between Los Angeles and Las Vegas. He earned his nickname because he had a reputation for 'going bugs' and striking out quickly when angered, but disliked it immensely and preferred friends to call him Ben. Anyone unlucky enough to use 'Bugsy' was likely to get a thump... if not worse.

Siegel had first come West from the Eastern seaboard, where he'd begun his criminal career extorting money from Jewish pushcart peddlers in New York, then moved on to bootlegging and racketeering, with instructions to develop illegal trade in California. He took his orders to heart and began setting up gambling dens, gambling ships (beyond the 12-mile coastal limit, and therefore legal floating casinos), drug dealing and other forms of smuggling, while getting to know some of Hollywood's biggest celebrities. Tall and good-looking, with piercing blue eyes, dark hair and natural charm, he looked like a movie version of a gangster himself. Siegel is also notorious for organising the first reliable nationwide bookmakers' wire service.

In 1945, funded by Mob money, he went into partnership with Billy Wilkerson to build the super-luxurious Flamingo Hotel and Casino in Vegas, at a cost of nearly $6m (four times the original budget). At the time it was the most sumptuous hotel Vegas had ever seen, with air-conditioning in every room and two swimming pools. Much of the 'overspend' was in fact being deposited by Siegel's girlfriend, Virginia Hill, in bank accounts across Switzerland and when Siegel's old business partner and ex-Murder Inc member Meyer Lansky found out, he sent henchmen to Las Vegas to see what was up.

On 20 June 1947, Siegel was killed by a barrage of bullets fired through the window of the lounge at his palatial Beverly Hills home. No one was ever arrested for the killing, but most biographers agree that Siegel was the victim of a Mob hit. Moments after his execution, Maurice Rosen and Gus Greenbaum, two of Lansky's associates with experience of casino management, entered the Flamingo and calmly informed staff that they were now in charge.

CARD SHARP

Poker is a game of silent courage and sublimated paranoia.
Al Reinert in *Texas Monthly* (1973)

WHAT YOU SEE...

Playing cards come in all shapes and sizes, with all manner of decoration. And while poker is normally played with very well-known brands of cards, to avoid cheating, you might like to consider using the Pro Deck Poker Champions deck as an alternative, if you can get your hands on one. Each card features a photo of a well-known player – perhaps to remind you to keep your poker face in place. They've been out of print for some years, but do turn up on card specialist sites and auction sites for just a few dollars.

POKER FOOD

Sticky Fingers

Whatever food you serve while playing poker, always remember to hand out plenty of paper napkins, or you'll wind up with greasy smears on your cards. No one's ever been accused of trying to mark their cards with mayonnaise, but there's always a first time!

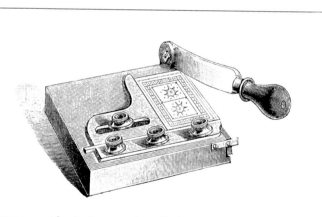

A common resort for cheats was to chop off a tiny curved piece off certain cards using special guillotines – you can't help but think many card players must have been pretty unobservant not to notice bits cut off their cards.

WOMEN OF POKER

Jennifer Harman

Jennifer Harman began playing poker for money at the age of eight, so no wonder she's full of confidence when she sits down to play for a million dollars, even though physically she is small and slight and deceptively soft looking. She began playing when her father, losing a game at home, would get her to sit in for him as a little kid. She usually won, and she still thinks being a woman gives her an advantage, stating in a recent interview: 'In general, most men don't think women can play. So, what often happens is that they try to run over me. They bluff their money off to me. I guess they see me as a meek little girl and think that I'm easily bluffed. I'm not!'

She turned pro at the age of 21 and slowly began to work her way up through the ranks, moving cautiously from low-limit games to higher limits... then dropping back down if she had a run of bad luck, all the time building her bankroll and investing money for the future. Now Harman is a seasoned player (often described as the best female poker player in the world) with seven stints at the WSOP final tables, and two WSOP bracelets to her name, one for deuce-to-seven lowball and one for limit hold 'em. So skilled is she at limit hold 'em that Doyle Brunson, when revamping his legendary poker manual *Super System*, asked her to write the chapter on it.

Nowadays she often plays very high cash games at the Bellagio in Las Vegas, choosing her battles carefully, and seems to prefer such play to tournaments, although she is starting to appear at more WSOP events. 'In a cash game, you always just make your decision based on the way the hand was played and your read of your opponents,' she says. 'In tournaments, there is so much other stuff to think about, like conserving chips, avoiding marginal situations, playing aggressively against short stacks and so on. They are just so different.'

CARD SHARP

Poker is a microcosm of all we admire and disdain about capitalism and democracy. It can be rough-hewn or polished, warm or cold, charitable and caring or hard and impersonal. It is fickle and elusive, but ultimately it is fair, and right, and just.
Lou Krieger, writer on poker

PRESIDENTIAL PLAYER

'Ike' Eisenhower was taught to play poker as a boy by an old Kansas woodsman named Bob Davis. Unlike other Presidents, Eisenhower did not like to play for significant stakes. With Davis, he recalled: 'We played for matches, and whenever my box of matches was exhausted, I'd have to roll in my blankets and go to sleep.'

While still a colonel, before the Second World War, Eisenhower resumed the habit of playing cards, taking on George Patton at poker twice a week.

GOOD CAUSE

Thaddeus Stevens, an anti-slavery campaigner, was known to be the best poker player in Washington. One night, having cleaned out several pro-slavery congressmen at an all-night game, he was approached by a black clergyman seeking contributions for his church. Stevens handed over all his winnings, saying reverently: 'God moves in mysterious ways.'

THE ROBIN HOOD OF POKER

While some players become millionaires from playing poker, one is content to give away his not inconsiderable tournament income. It's no wonder, therefore, that father of six Barry Greenstein is known as 'the Robin Hood of Poker'.

A maths graduate who used to write software for Symantec, Greenstein puts his mathematical brain to work on the theory of poker – he's the author of *Ace on the River* and is well known as tutor to Mimi Tran, who in return for poker tips taught him to speak Vietnamese. Greenstein has won several major tournaments, including Larry Flynt's Poker Challenge Cup in 2003, where he netted the million-dollar first prize at seven-card stud, and the Jack Binion World Poker Open in 2004 – first place there gave him $1,278,370 for a range of charities he supports, including Children Inc. He's extremely well regarded by other players and, as Chris Ferguson put it after losing out in the 2004 WSOP Deuce-to-Seven Lowball tournament: 'Barry may very well be the top player in the world right now. All the top players respect Barry. I never like to lose, but if you are going to lose to anyone, who's better to lose to than Barry, since all the money is going to charity?'

POKER CLOTHING

For years, poker players resisted the lure of high fashion. The problem of concealing tells from other players while surviving 20-hour marathon sessions dictated a wardrobe dominated by large hats, dark glasses and the sort of chavtastic shell-suits modelled by several famous professionals.

These days, however, the plethora of televised tournaments have prompted poker aces to take their attire more seriously. Many online gaming sites sell extensive ranges of clothing. Here is the pick of high-stakes high fashion:

Card Player blue hoodie
'A fashion "must-have" for today's poker player,' the Card Player catalogue insists. 'Impress your friends and create a winning table image for yourself when you wear this Card Player Navy Blue Hooded Sweatshirt with comfortable, full athletic cut.' Guaranteed to bring a touch of urban menace to any table – and the oversized hood helps with your poker face.
www.CardPlayer.com

Eye glasses
Disconcerting poker shades designed so that all your opposition sees staring back at them is a pair of strange-looking eyes emblazoned on the lenses. One eye is open, the other winking for maximum disconcerting effect.
www.gamblersgeneralstore.com

Hawaiian-style poker shirt
Take fashion victimhood to a whole new level with this cotton-rayon short-sleeved shirt emblazoned with brighter-than-bright chip- and card-related designs. Plus sizes available.
www.poker-wear.com

One for the ladies
Taste-free 'Got the Nuts?' women's T-shirt from LadiesHoldem Online Store – purveyors of 'cute and fun poker clothing, made for women by women.' Also available: 'Stacked', 'Size Does Matter', 'Take me to the River' and 'Real Women Go All In' designs.
www.cafepress.com/ladiesholdem

Madhatter Ace top hat
We pretty much guarantee opponents will underestimate anyone brave enough to turn up at the table sporting this ridiculous piece of attire. The 18in-high plush top hat is made from black and red velvet, and has garish panels depicting the four suits. Weighs nearly 1lb. Fully lined and adjustable.
www.thetreebuilder.com

POKER PLAYERS YOU CAN HIRE

Whether it's a master class, after-dinner speaking or product endorsement you're looking for, here's a list of people signed up with 'All American Speakers' who are ready to take your dollar (or pound, or yen, or Euro...)

1. Phil 'Poker Brat' Hellmuth Jr
2. Annie 'Duchess of Poker' Duke
3. Daniel 'Kid Poker' Negreanu
4. Antonio 'The Magician' Esfandiari
5. Evelyn 'Evybabee' Ng
6. David 'D Dub' Williams
7. Erick 'E-Dog' Lindgren
8. Phil 'The Truth' Darden
9. Phil 'Unabomber' Laak
10. Gus 'The Great Dane' Hansen

ON EDGE: WAYS OF DISTRACTING YOUR OPPONENTS

There are all sorts of things you can do to distract your opponents, to intimidate or to mislead them, and the first place to start is with your body.

Razzle Dazzle I
Flashy jewellery with lots of rocks, and anything that picks up the light, can form a visual distraction for the players sitting opposite. So bring on the bling!

Razzle Dazzle II
People don't like to see clashing colours; it disrupts them on a sub-conscious level because orange, hot pink and custard yellow were just not meant to be bedfellows. Visit a Hawaiian shirt shop before tournaments.

Sweet Smell of Success I
Overpowering aftershave (or body odour) can put the best of us off our game. This type of distraction can be particularly useful during hay-fever season or if your opponents suffer from allergies.

Sweet Smell of Success II
People who suffer from foot odour – you know who you are – could do worse than to slip off their shoes during a long match.

HALL OF FAME

During the 1980s, even more colourful characters were added to the Poker Hall of Fame at Binion's Horseshoe.

1986 – Henry Green

Another road gambler, Green was known for his even temper, pleasant manner and facility of playing all forms of poker.

1987 – Walter Clyde 'Puggy' Pearson

A seven-card stud aficionado, Pearson is considered the father of the poker tournament since he first broached the idea. The cigar-chomping Tennessee-born player won the world title in 1973 and still lives and plays professionally in Vegas. His even style of play, betting only when he has a good hand, is well known among other players, but outside of the game he's known for his homespun wisdom.

POKER PUZZLER

Fit the following terms into these phrases – but only use them once each!

A POCKET	**E** ANTE
B RIVER	**F** TILT
C BLIND	**G** BLUFF
D FLUSH	**H** FLOP

1. In the Christian faith things that happened before the first Council of Nice are known as _____-Nicene.

2. Hunters often spend time in a _____ waiting for their prey.

3. In computer science, another term for a floating point operation is a _____.

4. An American slang term for being in prison is up the _____.

5. A _____ is a canopy that can shade a boat, wagon or cart.

6. Very steep, almost vertical promentaries or cliffs are known as _____s.

7. If you don't duck fast enough in some sports, you could wind up with a ball hitting you _____ in the face.

8. Grain and metal ore can both be stored in a _____.

Answers on page 153.

POKER IN PROSE

In 1979, poker pro Bobby Hoff squared off at the final table of the World Series of Poker against six other world-class players and Hal Fowler, a no-name PR man from Los Angeles. Fowler was in by far the worst position, having only about $2,000 in chips out of the $550,000 at the table, but after a marathon 12-hour final head-to-head, the PR man won the tournament, the first amateur ever to do so. Fowler went back to LA and never played big-stakes poker again. As for Hoff – 20 years later, he could still hardly believe he had lost.

I got about as tough a beat as you'll ever hear about in a key hand that came up just before the final hand. With one card to come, I had two queens and a six kicker; Hal had two jacks with a king kicker. He had all his money in the pot, and I still had $150,000 in chips. He caught a king on the river to make two pair, kings and jacks. Nobody even remembers that hand. In the final pot, I raised with two aces and Hal called me with 7-6 offsuit. The flop came J-3-5. I bet half my money on the flop and he called the bet. Hal caught a four on the turn to make the gutshot straight and win the title.

Lady luck was on his side that day. Eric Drache (the tournament director) estimated that Hal took 20 Valiums just while we were playing head-up. I won all of the little pots, but every time we had a big confrontation and a big pot, Hal won every single one. After each of those pots except the last one, I came back and was in the tournament again.

Having Hal beat me in the World Series of Poker had a big effect on my life. I had nightmares for three weeks afterward. I never realised how much I wanted to win until I got down there with a chance to win it. In my life, I've been in many tough spots – I've bluffed my money many times, and I've had a huge amount of rushes. But never have the palms of my hands sweated, except for that one time at the final table. I thought I was playing for the money, but then I realised that I wanted to win it. I still get quite emotional when I talk about it.

Dana Smith, Tom McEvoy and Ralph Wheeler, *The Championship Table at the World Series of Poker* (2004)

TELL IT AS IT IS

Poker players act. Of course. Exaggerated mannerisms – shrugs, exasperation – are usually fairly transparent attempts at deception. If one of your opponents is going out of their way to convey the impression that they've got an iffy hand, be sure you'll need great cards to call them successfully. Conversely, few if any of the players you meet will be thinking about their breathing. Changes in breathing patterns are one of the clearest tells you can ever hope to spot. Opponents with strong hands will be excited and that means they'll tend to breathe faster; those who are bluffing often hold their breath or seem exaggeratedly calm.

CARD MARKING THE OLD FASHIONED WAY

The earliest sharps seem to have marked cards by raising tiny burrs along the edges with a fingernail. But this crude technique was far too easily detected, and it was superseded in the early nineteenth century by pricking the corners of cards with a little needle, often concealed in the base of a ring. Gamblers would surreptitiously prick all the court cards that passed through their hands, not so much in order to be able to identify them in an opponent's hand as to make them noticeable when dealing. Court cards could then be retained and dealt to the sharp or a confederate using the technique of 'second dealing'.

A few years later, a far more subtle technique, involving shading the backs of cards with smudges of dye, was developed. American sharps used a special paste, carried in a specially made 'shading box', which could be sewn into the lining of a jacket. A finger passed across the tiny slot in the shading box would pick up a tiny smudge of paste that could be transferred to a card. Careful placement of the smudge would make it possible to tell exactly what card an opponent held. Sharps generally carried two shading boxes, one filled with red paste and the other with blue, allowing them to mark almost any card imperceptibly. The marks deposited could also be instantly removed with a single rub if suspicions were aroused.

'It is worthy of note,' one nineteenth-century treatise on card marking observes, 'that these boxes are considered to be so good that they are not included in the catalogues of dealers in so-called "sporting goods". They are kept as a secret among those who are "in the know".'

FINDING YOUR WAY AROUND POKER TOWN

Betts Street, E1
Casino Avenue, SE24
Champion Hill, SE5
Chance Street, E2
Chip Street, SW4
Deck Close, SE16
Fortune Way, NW10
Fourth Avenue, NE24
Gambole Road, SW17
Games Road, EN4
Kingscourt Road, SW16
Leader Avenue, E12
Queen Square, WC1
Playfair Mansions, W14
River Lane, TW10
The Straight, Southall
Tell Grove, SE22

CARD SHARP

*Poker exemplifies the worst aspects of capitalism
that have made our country so great.*
Walter Matthau, actor

NO CHANGE

Playing poker for huge stakes brings its own problems for the high rollers of the game. Photographer Ulvis Alberts, at the World Series of Poker to shoot portraits of leading players for his book *Poker Face*, was approached by several of his subjects with requests for prints. Alberts explained the cost was $75 per picture. 'But,' the photographer recalled, 'suddenly there was a problem. Nobody had change. So I charged them $100 and everyone was happy.'

UGLY FLAMINGO

In the early 1970s, the Flamingo, in Las Vegas, was the place to go for poker action – what there was of it. The casino's five-table card room was under the auspices of Johnny Moss, who kept a pistol in his top drawer and set aside three of his tables for what were known as 'snatch games': dubious tourist traps in which dealers were instructed to 'rake' a huge proportion of each pot as the house's take. Casinos were not required to inform players of the size of their rake at this time, and Moss's dealers routinely creamed off 75% of the cash gambled at their tables. When the Gaming Control Board finally made it a legal requirement to post the rake, Moss responded by making up a sign reading: **RAKE: ZERO TO 100 PERCENT**.

POKER PUZZLER

Which of the following is NOT a name for three of a kind in different versions of poker?
a) Run
b) Trips
c) Set
d) Rolled up
Answer on page 153.

POKER IN PROSE

[Gambling] was *the* amusement – *the* grand occupation of most classes – apparently the life and soul of the place... The extensive saloons, in each of which a dozen... tables might be placed, were continually crowded, and around the tables themselves the players often stood in lines three or four deep, everyone vieing with his neighbors for the privilege of reaching the board, and staking his money as fast as the wheel and ball could be rolled or the card turned... Judges and clergymen, physicians and advocates, merchants and clerks... tradesmen, mechanics and laborers, miners and farmers, all adventurers in their kind – every one elbowed his way to the gaming-table, and unblushingly threw down his golden or silver stake.

The Annals of San Francisco (1854)

IT'S YOUR LOSS

In 1996, US gamblers were willing to risk more than $500bn, and lost over $116bn of it. Of that $116bn, around $49bn went to various casinos. Here's what happened to the rest:

Indian gaming sites **9%**
State lotteries **33%**
Pari-mutuel racetracks and jai alai **8%**
Bingo, card rooms and charitable games **7%**
Bookmakers **1%**

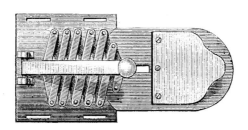

Gamblers who used these lazy tongues, designed to be inserted up your sleeve to whisk away unwanted cards and substitute aces, were liable to be caught out if they pressed the lever at the wrong moment and punched an opponent in the stomach when they meant to shake hands.

FISHMONGER'S HALL

The most notorious gambler in England 200 years ago was William Crockford. Born above his father's fish shop in Temple Bar, just outside the City of London, Crockford was brought up in poverty and enjoyed a negligible education. 'Coarse in his habits, dirty in his person, fat, flabby and pallid, foul of mouth and without any sort of refinement,' this master gambler nonetheless possessed a natural genius for calculating odds that stood him in good stead in his chosen career. By 1828, his wealth was such that he was able to open a gaming club opposite Whites on St James's Street, so sumptuous that it was patronised by the wealthiest aristocrats in England. The attractions of Crockford's were its superb elegance and social exclusivity – it was harder to become a member there than at any other club in London – exquisite food (provided by Louis Eustache Ude, who had once been chef to Napoleon Bonaparte), and what were, at the time, the highest limits in the world.

Crockford, it is said, made it his business to investigate the pedigrees and expectations of every aristocrat in England, and he knew almost to the hour when the country's wealthiest heirs expected to come into their fortunes. Play at his club was so deep that well in excess of £20,000 (a huge sum for the time) was won and lost there on some nights.

Most of the players privately despised Crockford, their social inferior. They called him 'The Fishmonger' behind his back and dubbed his club 'Fishmonger's Hall'. But the canny gambler had his revenge, for during Crockford's 15-year existence, he took so much money from his members that several of Britain's noblest families have still not recovered from the losses their ancestors incurred at the club.

Crockford met his doom in betting heavily on the infamous Derby of 1844, 'which contained more intrigue, roguery, double-crossing and deception than any race since that day.' The horse he had backed with much of his fortune was nobbled and Britain's greatest-ever gambler died two days later, it was said, of a broken heart. He should have stuck to poker.

CARD SHARP

In the beginning, everything was even money.
Mike Caro, poker psychologist

'WHERE'S THE ACTION IN ANDALUCIA?'

The number of casinos currently operating in selected European countries, according to the World Casino Directory:

England	75	Portugal	8
Russia	73	Denmark	6
Germany	51	Italy	4
Spain	16	Wales	3
Scotland	14	Eire	1
Holland	12	Vatican City	0
Bulgaria	9		

NO SEX PLEASE, WE'RE GAMBLERS

Small talk, hobbies and pretty much everything else are in short supply in the Las Vegas home of poker doyen Doyle Brunson, if his pals are to be believed. 'He wants to play poker and he wants to eat,' Brunson's business partner Dewey Tomko says of his old friend. 'He doesn't want to do nothing else.'

MOSS THE MAGNIFICENT

In 1939, Johnny Moss won quarter of a million dollars playing poker against newly-rich oil barons during one of Texas's booms. He came back from the game uplifted, and told his wife Virgie to go out and find the nicest home in Dallas.

So off went Virgie and one of her friends to the realtors' offices, where they looked at dozens of properties. After numerous viewings of places that were good, but not quite good enough – he had said to pick the best after all, money no limit – and after two weeks she finally found her dream home and came home excitedly to tell Moss to get the money ready.

'You should've looked faster,' he told her with typical sang froid. In the two weeks he'd hit a run of bad luck and lost every dollar and cent of it.

THE BIGGEST GAME IN TOWN

Born in the 1960s and played more or less non-stop ever since, the world's biggest poker game has moved around Las Vegas over time, from the Dunes to the Mirage, the Golden Nugget and finally the Bellagio – but always featured the same shifting nucleus of players. Though invariably based around a 'live one' (a wealthy amateur looking for the thrill of facing off against the world's top players), vacationers drifting past the Big Game can expect to see at least half a dozen sweatsuit-clad aces spitballing their way through $4,000/$8,000 hands of hold 'em, Omaha, seven-card stud and triple-draw. 'Live ones' dealt in to the game have included porn baron Larry Flynt, the World Poker Tour's multimillionaire backer Lyle Berman, and Rene Angelil, husband of Celine Dion. Most days the pros are drawn from this stellar roster:

Bobby Baldwin	Former world champion hall-of-famer
Doyle Brunson	Two-time world champion hold 'em legend
Johnny Chan	Two-time world champion, famed poker bully
Phil Ivey	World's top 20-something cash game poker stud
Chip Reese	Renowned as the best all-round poker player in the world

Feeling lucky? Baldwin and the others welcome all comers. There's just one snag. Buying your way into the Big Game will cost you a minimum $500,000 per session.

VARIETIES OF POKER

Seven-Card Stud

Seven-card stud is the most popular variety of stud poker, and has been since the 1860s. Players are dealt three concealed ('down') cards and then four more exposed cards, one by one. There are five rounds of betting and thus plenty of action; the most important thing, experts say, is never to enter a pot unless your three hole cards can work together, because you can be sure that at least one of your opponents will be able to improve their hand as their four exposed cards are dealt. Seven-card stud aficionados like the fact that almost any hand can be drawn and played – in Texas hold 'em, they point out, full houses and four of a kind become possible only when the board contains at least one pair.

DANGEROUS GAMES

Playing poker could be a pretty dangerous business as late as the mid 1950s. Doyle Brunson, who got his start as a hustler around 1955, witnessed five murders playing on Fort Worth's Exchange Avenue, including one in which a player at the table next to him had his brains spattered over the wall in an argument over a girl. He was also robbed three times at gunpoint, once at knifepoint, and beaten up on more than one occasion. 'By the time I was 40,' Brunson says of his back-room game, 'everyone but me and one other guy were either dead or in the penitentiary.'

CELEBRITY POKER – THE 'A' LIST

Big-name celebrities who play with the pros – and sometimes beat them!

Patrick Brunel – French singer and actor who holds a bracelet for the 1998 WSOP $5,000 Limit Hold 'em tournament.

Ben Affleck – California State Poker Championship winner and WSOP finalist.

Tobey Maguire – has won the Phil Hellmuth Poker Invitational and is 940th on the WSOP all-time list.

James Woods – has his own online poker room with Vince Van Patten **www.hollywoodpoker.com**

Jennifer Tilly – won the Ladies Texas No Limit Hold 'em Event at 2005's WSOP.

Matt Damon – WSOP Texas Hold 'em finalist, got the bug while studying card players for his role in *Rounders* with Ed Norton.

Ed Norton – WSOP Texas Hold 'em finalist. Coincidentally Norton made a name for himself in *The People vs Larry Flynt*.

Mimi Rogers – Tom Cruise's ex is a regular participant in the WSOP and other tournaments.

Penn Gillette – the big half of Penn and Teller, WSOP entrant and frequent flyer in celebrity poker matches.

Caprice – plays weekly tournaments on **paradisepoker.com**, and played the Legends of Poker tournament in Los Angeles.

Laura Prepon – star of *That '70s Show*, producer of *E!*'s poker show, played in the 2004 World Series and finished about 450th, and plays daily.

ANOTHER WORLD

Playing for years at the highest stakes does leave its mark on even the most level-headed players, and many find it very hard to adjust to real-world issues such as the price of milk. A story told of Eric Drache, the urbane Vegas card-room manager and noted stud player, illustrates this nicely. Drache was on the receiving end of a beating in a tough afternoon session when he was paged and asked to take an urgent phone call from his wife, Jane, who had been in a car accident. The following conversation ensued:

Eric: Are you hurt?
Jane: No.
Eric: Is anyone else hurt?
Jane: No.
Eric: That's all right, then.
Jane: But I've done $1,500 worth of damage to the side of the car.
Eric: Then call the insurance.
Jane: But $1,500 damage to our beautiful Jaguar!
Eric: Honey, I'm stuck four beautiful Jaguars at the moment. Call the insurance.

IT'S OFFICIAL

No longer a maverick game, Poker now has a host of governing bodies that lay down the law when it comes to how, when and where play occurs.

Online Players Association – www.casinogazette.com
International Poker Federation – www.ipfpoker.com
International Association of Professional Poker Players (IAPPP) – www.iappp.net
American Gaming Association (AGA) – www.americangaming.org
National Indian Gaming Association – www.indiangaming.org
British Casino Association (BCA) – www.britishcasinoassociation.org.uk
Tournament Directors' Association – www.thepokerforum.com/tda
Interactive Gambling, Gaming and Betting Association – www.iggba.org.uk
Worshipful Company of Makers of Playing Cards –
www.makersofplayingcards.co.uk
International Playing Card Association – i-p-c-s.org

CARD SHARP

Nobody is always a winner, and anybody who says he is,
is either a liar or doesn't play poker.
Amarillo Slim, poker player

POKER IN PROSE

Titanic Thompson was a legendary poker ace and golf hustler – playing the latter game off scratch both left- and right-handed – who got his nickname because it was widely if incorrectly rumoured that he had survived the 1912 sinking of the famous liner. His former partner, Byron 'Cowboy' Wolford, the renowned rodeo champion, recalls one of the gambler's most notorious scams:

Ty had a deal back then where he'd be sitting around poker places that he'd never been to before and he'd say, 'Guys, I know this woman who's a psychic. I'll tell you how good she is: You take a card out of that deck and put it on the table in front of us. She doesn't live in this state, but I'll bet you that if you go call her, she'll tell you what the card is.' Well, back then there wasn't any TV, no shortwave stuff, and Ty had been right there with them all the time, hadn't gone anywhere. Might near anybody would go for that deal.

So, he bet $1,000 that they could call this woman who was a psychic and she could tell them over the telephone exactly what that card was. Then somebody would take a card out and put it on the table. 'Okay,' he'd say, 'here's the long distance number. Just ask for Miss Brown.' They'd call and say, 'Is Miss Brown there?'

'Just a moment,' someone would answer. In a minute another voice said 'Hello?'

'Miss Brown, we're down here in so-and-so and we've got a bet on. This gentleman says you're quite a psychic.'

'I think I am,' she'd say.

'Well, we've taken a card out of the deck and laid it in the middle of the table and he bet that you could tell us what card it is.' She'd answer, 'Give me a moment.' After a short pause, she'd say, 'The four of diamonds.' And the guy would almost faint. Of course, Ty had a different name for every card in the deck. If it was the four of diamonds, he'd tell them to ask for Miss Brown. It if was the nine of hearts, it might be Miss Ruby.

Dana Smith, Tom McEvoy and Ralph Wheeler, *The Championship Table at the World Series of Poker* (2004)

EIGHT THINGS TO CONSIDER BEFORE TURNING PRO

OK, you have a decent, solid game, clean up more often than not in your home game, and maybe win some money online, too. But do you really have what it takes to turn pro? Poker writers Lou Krieger and Richard Harroch offer this advice to would-be professionals.

1. Poker isn't like most jobs

Sure, there are upsides to being a pro card player. You're your own boss, you choose the hours you work and the potential rewards are getting bigger every day. But there's no salary, no guarantee you'll have a steady income – and how many other jobs carry the risk of actually losing money? Most novice pros go bust less than 12 months into their careers.

2. Consider your own results

Keep records, and keep them up to date. You're not going to improve if you don't know what you did, and how you did when you did it.

3. Don't play when you're not at your best

If you're not feeling confident and ready to play, don't. It will cost you far less to take in dinner and a movie than endure a losing session at the table.

4. Decide where to play

Chances are there isn't going to be enough action where you live to keep you and your family alive. Most poker pros live in Vegas, California or Atlantic City; the rest just travel an awful lot. Sooner or later you're going to have to consider moving to a gambling hot spot, but before you do – check your prospective new home out. Go and stay there for four to six weeks, not so much to take in the ambience as to find out if you're going to cut it playing for more money against better players.

5. Use statistics to establish expectations

Successful poker means treading the fine line between playing aggressively enough to maximise your winnings and not taking unnecessary risks. A firm grasp of statistics will help you make the right decisions.

6. Assess your risk tolerance

Are you planning to grind out a living taking few risks in a $10-$20 game, or go for broke playing aggressively for higher stakes? Risking it all will be a lot more exciting, but you're bound to go broke more than once along the way.

7. Follow good examples

Poker is a solitary profession. You can make it more bearable by finding a mentor, another player you can trust and learn from. Look at pros you admire, try to work out why they are successful, and above all treasure the friendships of those you can trust to tell you the truth about your game.

8. Ask the right questions

Take responsibility for your own performance at the card table. Don't ask: 'Why do I always get bad beats?' Do ask: 'What can I do to improve my game?'

CARD SHARP

Limit poker is a science, but no-limit is an art. In limit, you are shooting at a target. In no-limit, the target comes alive and shoots back at you.
Crandall Addington, poker player

VARIETIES OF POKER

Chinese Poker

If you ever chance across a couple of pros whiling away a few hours at a table between major games, chances are you'll find them playing Chinese poker. The game can be a good way of passing time, because it depends almost entirely on luck and so money will pass more or less evenly between two players over time. Players are dealt 13 cards and have to arrange them into three poker hands – two of five cards and one of three. Hands are ranked and awarded points, and the trick is to score more points than your opponents. The element of luck in Chinese poker is so great, in fact, that the game was thrown out of the World Series of Poker just a year after its debut.

2005 WORLD SERIES OF POKER: THE FACTS

Total number of registered entrants:		5,661
Online qualifiers refused admittance because they were underage:		10
Registered players whose $10,000 buy-in money got 'lost in the post':		13
Online qualifiers who died before the big event:		2
Number of bloggers covering the entire WSOP:		10
Bloggers covering the main event:		30
Prize pool for the first 39 events in the World Series (combined):		$52,000,000
Prize pool for the main event (no-limit hold 'em):		$52,818,610
Main event prize money:	1st	$7,500,000
	2nd	$4,250,000
	3rd	$2,000,000
Amount donated by the WSOP to charity Meals on Wheels:		$1,000,000

EARLY POKER SONGS

In terms of song, poker and sex seem to go hand in hand, even though in reality the game can be very sexless. Fleetwood Mac's 'Lazy Poker Blues' seems, at first, to suggest the protagonists are having a quiet day with some 'lazy poker goin' on'. It's only when the singer notes that his partner's going to keep his poker warm that the song shifts into a much more sensual mode.

One of the best early songs with a poker theme is Bluesman T-Bone Walker's 'You're My Best Poker Hand'. It starts off sweetly enough, saying 'I need a queen like you to make my hand OK' as it describes, verse by verse, a poker game,

culminating in 'his face turned pale when he saw my queen high flush'.

Poker gets surprisingly few mentions in American music hall and burlesque songs, possibly because it was less well known than we might imagine among the populace, and on the stage there are very few references – Jerome Kern's 1906 'Poker Duet' from the review show The Rich Mr Hoggenheimer is an exception. Charlotte Blake copywrited 'That Poker Rag' in 1909, and novelty songs like 1919's mildly risqué 'Who Played Poker with Pocahontas When John Smith Went Away?' provide further clues to the game's familiarity.

WOMEN OF POKER

Annie Duke

Annie Duke is known as a sphinx-like player with an almost unreadable face. First taught by her brother, Howard 'The Professor' Lederer, she took to the game swiftly and gave up her doctoral degree course (in psycholinguistics, to add to her degree in psychology and English) in order to pursue poker professionally.

Her favoured game is Omaha high-low, and she holds a WSOP bracelet for winning the 2004 $2000 high-low event – the previous year she came sixth. But she's also been successful playing limit hold 'em, taking several second places at the WSOP. Other high-profile wins include coming first at the 2004 ESPN World Series of Poker Tournament of Champions and second at the Bellagio Five-Star World Poker Classic in the Omaha tournament.

The Bellagio's her natural home, with its high-stakes tables. She and her husband and four children live in Vegas and enjoy her winnings. One of a handful of star female players, Duke gained notoriety in the last couple of years for tutoring actor Ben Affleck, who went on to win and place in several tournaments after heeding her wisdom.

I KNEW THEM WHEN...

Former jobs of some poker pros:

Doyle Brunson	Office supply salesman
Johnny Chan	Short order chef
TJ Cloutier	Oil rig worker
Chris Ferguson	Working towards a PhD in Artificial Intelligence
Barry Greenstein	Computer programmer
Jennifer Harman	Cocktail waitress
Tony Holden	Prince Charles's authorised biographer
Chris Moneymaker	Accountant
Men Nguyen	Bus driver
Dewey Tomko	Kindergarten teacher
Dave Ulliott	Jeweller

*Beau Brummell used to say that the tailor shouldn't make the man.
In this case, the tailor makes the winner!*

THE DUCHESS OF FOURTH STREET

Poker was introduced to the UK – according to WJ Florence in his *Handbook on Poker* (1891) – by General Robert Schenck, who was the American ambassador in the early 1870s. Schenck was spending the weekend at a country pile in Somerset owned by the Duke and Duchess of W— (as the author puts it, with maddeningly Victorian inexactitude) when the conversation turned to card games. 'During this talk,' the writer continued,' he described to [the Duchess] the beauties of poker in such a way that she became intensely interested, and begged him to write her out a set of rules and directions for playing the great American game. This Mr Schenck very kindly did. The Duchess learned to play poker, and as it wove its fascinating toils about her she wanted her friends to learn also. For convenience she had Mr Schenck's letter printed in a neat pamphlet and distributed among her friends of the court circles.'

TELL IT AS IT IS

According to Poker-tells guru, Mike Caro, one of the biggest giveaways you're likely to spot at the table is the player who instinctively glances at their pile of chips immediately after receiving their cards. Those who do this almost invariably have good hands, or have just received a card that significantly strengthens their position. 'In some games,' Caro says, 'average players could be big winners if they did nothing but look for this tell and play their normal game.'

POKER PUZZLER

You have a pair of pocket aces in your hand, playing against one opponent, and the flop so far is 6♠ 4♥ 7♦ 9♣. You are waiting for the final card of the flop. What is your chance of winning the hand?

a) 99%
b) 95%
c) 75%
d) 50%

Answer on page 153.

A BLUE ONE

Herbert Bayard Swope, the most famous newspaperman in America between the two World Wars, was a renowned host through whose Long Island home many of the biggest names of the 1920s, 1930s and 1940s passed. A fanatical poker player, Swope regularly presided over a school where the participants included heavyweight politician Bernard Baruch, Harold Ross, founder of the *New Yorker*, renowned wit Alexander Woolcott, and Harpo Marx. The stakes were remarkably high and caught many of Swope's guests by surprise. On one occasion, when David O Selznick agreed to sit in on a session, the big-shot Hollywood producer tried to intimidate the table, telling Swope: 'I'm not interested in any of your little games. When I play poker, I like to shoot the works. Give me $10,000 of chips.' Baruch stifled a yawn, turned to Swope and said, in a bored voice: 'You're banking, Herb. Go ahead. Throw him a blue one.'

THE COMEBACK KING

The 1982 World Series of Poker saw perhaps the most remarkable comeback in the history of the game. 'Treetop' Jack Straus (a former college basketball player who stood well over six feet tall) had been down to his last $500 of chips earlier in the tournament, but battled his way through to the final table and a head-to-head with one-time kindergarten teacher Dewey Tomko. Come the final hand, Straus was dealt A♦ 10♣ to Tomko's A♦ 4♥. The flop came up 6♦ 5♠ 4♠, and both players went all in. Tomko was in the lead at this point and he held on at the turn when Q♠ was dealt. Only an ace or a 10 at the river could win the tournament for Straus, and crowds lined the table 25 deep to see the final card turned. It was 10♠. Straus's 9.2:1 ship had come in, and his hand — still one of the most famous played in WSOP history — won a then-record pot of $967,000.

POKER GOURMET

The Bellagio, as well as hosting some of the highest-rolling games, also offers some of the best food in Vegas, in no less than seven multi-award winning, gourmet restaurants. Choose from:

Le Cirque – a mix of classic and rustic French food in a silk-hung circular dining room that looks out onto dancing fountains.

Circo – more casual and gusty sibling to Le Cirque, decorated in an over-the-top ochre-and-bull's blood circus theme.

Prime Steakhouse – decked out as an Art Deco gentlemen's club, Prime is regularly voted best steak restaurant in Vegas.

Shintaro – a Californian-inspired Japanese restaurant (so it has bright Mexican-style tapestry cushions and a golden ambiance) with Sushi bar and an emphasis on 'Theatre Cooking' – well, what else do you expect in Vegas?

Picasso – original Picassos decorate the restaurant space, alongside chef Julian Serrano's many awards.

Michael Mina – innovative seafood with Californian influences

Jasmine – Cantonese, Szechuan and Hunan dishes in a bizarre satin-chaired, be-chandeliered environment.

HALL OF FAME

For the first time since 1979, in 1988, two people were found worthy of entry to the hallowed Poker Hall of Fame. And in 1990, founder of the Horseshoe Casino, Benny Binion, made it in himself.

1988 – Doyle Brunson

Winner of the world title in 1976 and 1977, Doyle Brunson is the first player to win a million in tournament play. His book *Super System: How I Made Over $1,000,000 Playing Poker* is considered the poker 'Bible'.

1988 – Jack Straus

Aggressive and very creative player who often risked everything on a bluff. World Series of Poker winner in 1982, he died in 1988 of a heart attack in the middle of a high-stakes game.

1989 – Fred 'Sarge' Ferris

Winner of the 1980 deuce-to-seven draw or Kansas city lowball world title in 1980, Ferris's most notorious game was the one in 1983 during which IRS agents raided the Horseshoe Casino in the middle of play and seized $46,000 of chips to pay his taxes.

1990 – Benny Binion

Founder of the Horseshoe Casino, home of the World Series of Poker, son of an itinerant horse trader who always ran high-stakes games and focused on play rather than entertainment in his casino to the end.

BUYING INTO A TOURNAMENT

Tournament play is what you see on TV, the form of the game that most novices are introduced to now. Because so many people enter each tournament, the ultimate prize from pooling all the entrance fees can be very high, but the cost of entering is comparatively low. Each player 'buys into' a tournament for the same set amount. If they drop out they can sometimes 're-buy' more chips at a later stage of the game, for a higher fee.

While major tournaments cost hundreds if not thousands of pounds to buy into, smaller ones may only cost £10 and are a great way to hone your skills. Online you can buy into tournaments for less than a dollar, and who knows, you may find yourself pitted against a world champion without ever knowing it.

GENEROUS TO A FAULT

Outside of the world of poker, if you say the name 'Kerry Packer', most of us still think of cricket. Australian media mogul Packer became infamous in the 1970s when, unable to get TV rights to the Test series, he created his own league, World Series Cricket, using his millions to buy the services of some of the best players in the world and in effect splitting the game in two until he got his way.

But within the gambling world he's known as the world's biggest casino gambler, once winning $26m at one sitting at the MGM Grand in Las Vegas, playing blackjack for $200,000 a hand. But what goes around comes around and he's rumoured to have lost £11m (then equivalent to $16.5m) at Crockfords in London in September 1999, as well as several other multimillion-dollar losses.

Legend has it that Packer's grandfather emigrated to the Australian mainland from Tasmania with the proceeds from a bet on the gee-gees – a neat idea, but completely unfounded. The Packer family's road to riches was mapped by Kerry Packer's father, who started by publishing women's magazines down under. Packer now has interests in several TV channels (including two he sold in 1987 for a billion dollars and bought back three years later for just $250m) and publishes 60% of magazines sold in Australia.

So it's no wonder he can afford to be generous; he's known in the world of casinos for giving $100,000 tips.

POKER ADVICE FROM JOHNNY MOSS

1. Nobody wins all the time, so when you lose, you need to learn what you can from it, then let it go. Forget it.
2. If you're afraid to lose your money, you can't play to win.
3. In order to learn any game, you have to find the best players and play with them.
4. In an otherwise even contest, the man with the best concentration will almost always win.

Don Jenkins, *Johnny Moss: Champion of Champions* (1981)

SONGS FOR GAMBLERS

'The Joker'...Steve Miller Band/Fatboy Slim
'Loser' ....Grateful Dead
'Hardin Wouldn't Run'...Johnny Cash
'Lost Highway' ....Hank Williams
'In the Jailhouse Now'..The Soggy Bottom Boys
'Desperado'...The Eagles
'Roving Gambler'...Simon and Garfunkel
'Rolling the Dice' ....Thunder
'Money Don't Matter Tonight' ....Prince
'Blues for Gamblers' ....Lightnin' Hopkins
'House of the Rising Sun' ....The Animals

CARD SHARP

If he be young and unskillful
Plays for shekels of silver and gold
Take his money my son praising Allah.
The fool was made to be sold.
Hafiz, Persian poet, fourteenth century

TOSS YOU FOR IT

High-rolling Australian businessman Kerry Packer probably dropped more money in Las Vegas than any man in history. Not surprisingly, casino bosses fell over themselves to keep him happy, comping him the best suites, his meals, and making sure he was surrounded at all times by a bevy of gorgeous girls.

Unsurprisingly, this treatment rankled with other guests, not least the wealthy Texan who one day came up to Packer, growling: 'What makes you so special? I've got $100m in the bank.'

'That's very impressive,' the Aussie billionaire shot back. 'I'll tell you what. I'll toss you for it.'

'You all look far too happy... you can't have lost anywhere near enough money yet.'

ROYAL POKER SLANG

Royal hands have their own particular slang – some are pretty obvious, some like 'gay waiter' a bit more obscure.

AK Walking Back to Houston

AQ Big Chick

AJ Ajax

KQ Marriage

KJ Kojak

K3 King crab

QT Quint

Q3 Gay waiter

J5 Jackson Five

The old nickname for AK, 'Walking Back to Houston', is so named because the hand proved the ruin of many old-time Texas gamblers who were tempted to play it, but ran into an opponent with a pair. Q3, 'Gay waiter' (otherwise known as a 'San Francisco Busboy') is so called because the card players' term for a three is 'trey' – hence 'Queen with a trey'.

LAS VEGAS: THE LATER YEARS

Las Vegas prospered in the 1950s and 1960s, with new casinos opening and the action beginning to move from Glitter Gulch to the Strip. But the town was heavily in thrall to the Mafia; casinos remained pretty seedy, and the entertainment still consisted of Italian lounge singers. No one would have called the Vegas of those days a family-friendly resort.

Things really began to change when the Stardust broke the unspoken crooners-only entertainment policy, bringing in the spectacular Lido de Paris floorshow from France. The show was a smash, running for a record-breaking 31 years.

That opened the floodgates. The Dunes brought in topless showgirls, and Circus Circus opened in 1968 – the first family resort in town. With its midway games, rides for kids and – more recently – an adjacent climate-controlled water park, it catered for holidaymakers and conventioneers as well as hardened gamblers.

The success of these resorts attracted the attention of major developers, and Steve Wynn's 3,000 rooms, $630m Mirage opened in the 1980s. It was followed by Treasure Island, next door, with its lagoon staging nightly sea battles.

The last two decades have seen the Mob eased out by more mega-resorts, each seemingly bigger and more costly than the last. The Excalibur, opened in 1990, has 4,000 rooms, a medieval castle and regular jousts; the pyramid-shaped Luxor boasts a full-scale reproduction of Tutankhamen's tomb, and the world's most powerful beam of light, blazing into the sky from its apex, is visible from 250 miles away. But even these extravaganzas are dwarfed by the MGM Grand, the largest resort hotel in the world, owned by billionaire Kirk Kerkorian.

Costing over $1bn and covering 112 acres, the Grand has a Hollywood theme, 5,000 rooms and – of course – a 171,500sq ft casino. Not to mention a 1,700-seat theatre, a 630-seat cinema, three pools and a 15,000-seat concert and sports arena.

With Elton John and Celine Dion alternating at Ceasar's Palace, 13 of the 20 largest resort hotels in the world, and room for well over 300,000 guests, modern-day Vegas is challenging Orlando as the number one tourist destination in the United States. Oh, and we hear there are a few poker tables dotted round the place as well.

THE POKER MILLIONAIRE CHALLENGE

After TV opened up appreciation of poker first in the UK and then in America, it was a bit of a no-brainer to mix flavour du jour reality TV with poker TV to produce a televised poker championship described as a 'unique... cross between the World Series of Poker and *Survivor*'.

There are 52 entrants who are selected via online applications and invited to the Plaza Hotel and Casino, Las Vegas, all expenses paid. Other entrants will qualify in regional tournaments with a maximum buy-in of $20, designed to ensure that almost any amateur poker player interested in participating gets a chance to try their luck. In total around 2,000 'Free Roll' seats will be available in addition to the cheap satellite entrants, and players will share around $2.5m in prize money. On the other hand, if you want to jump straight to the final tournament, you can buy into that for $5,000. If you fancy your chances, get over to
www.pokermillionairechallenge.com

POKER PUZZLER

What one Texas hold 'em hand will renowned gambler Doyle Brunson never play?
Answer on page 153.

NATURAL COMPETITORS

You might think that there are few lifestyles less healthy than that of a poker pro – long, mostly night-time, hours spent slumped in the same seat in a smoky casino. But a surprising number of top players are or were fine athletes.

Doyle Brunson – basketball scholarship, Hardin-Simmons University

Mike Sexton – gymnastics scholarship, Ohio State University

Jack Straus – basketball, Texas A&M University

Erick Lindgren – basketball scholarship, Butte Junior College, California

TJ Cloutier – football and baseball scholarship, University of California at Berkeley – he played in the Rose Bowl in 1959

Barry Greenstein – Varsity wrestler at his Chicago high school

STANDARDS

According to Bobby Baldwin, former world champ and now president of Las Vegas's high-stakes poker haven, the Bellagio Hotel, the most important thing any novice player has to do is develop a sense of standards, an instinctive understanding of what hands are worth playing in given circumstances.

During his first days in the game, Baldwin remembers: 'I was floating around, trying to figure out which hands were playable, which hands called for a raise, which hands should be thrown in. Without standards, you have to use 90% of your concentration deciding each time what to do with a given hand. All that mental energy should be devoted to your opponents and trying to decipher the small things which made this hand slightly different from familiar hands that you've seen in the past.'

CHIP OFF THE OLD BLOCK

Ace pro Chip Reese takes special pride in the steadiness of his game. That's why, asked to describe the greatest poker he ever played, he nominates a hideous session in the Big Game, fought for the highest stakes at Sam's Town in Vegas back in 2003.

An appalling run of duff cards and bad beats saw Reese down six figures every day. By the time the game broke up, he had taken losses of $2.5m. But that, he says, was because he had played the greatest poker of his life. 'I really believe,' he says, 'that if someone else had had my cards, they would have lost $7m.'

HENRY CLAY, THE GAMBLING PRESIDENTIAL HOPEFUL

Henry Clay, who ran for President in the election of 1832, was a swashbuckling high-stakes poker player who once won $40,000 in a single game and was renowned for bluffing. In one hand against Daniel Webster, Clay raised aggressively, Webster responding until there was $2,000 on the table. When Clay finally called, Webster smiled sheepishly and showed a pair of deuces. 'The pot is yours,' Clay laughed. 'I only have an ace high.'

PLAY IT BY THE RULES

Men 'The Master' Nguyen, a former Vietnamese boat person, who battled his way up to become one of Las Vegas's top pros, is unusual among professionals in travelling with a retinue. Men is a renowned mentor of aspiring poker aces, tutoring a posse of maths-savvy Vietnamese apprentices in the ways of the game. In exchange for receiving this stellar course of instruction, Men's students agree to abide by his tough code of conduct. The rules of the game:

- 2am curfew
- No drugs
- No chasing other players' girlfriends
- When Men tells you to do something, you do it

BIG BUCKS

The World Series of Poker is changing as the mushrooming number of entrants boosts prize money to unheard-of levels. Once it was big news if a tournament offered a million pounds in prize money to be split between all the placing players, let alone as a first prize. Now each year seems to bring a huge leap in the amount of money one lucky player – increasingly previously unheard-of players from outside the States, or even amateurs who play poker online only – walks away with. This year's champion Joseph Hatchem, although he'd been playing poker professionally in Australia for three years, was unknown on the poker circuit outside Oz. He automatically becomes the biggest-ever winner in WSOP history with a $7.5m first prize. In fact, the last nine finishers all got more than a million dollars each.

Last year's world champion, Greg 'Fossilman' Raymer, is the second-highest WSOP earner ever with a grand total of $5,234,794, earned over three tournaments. But he's beaten by David Williams, who's trousered around $7m in the WSOP – half of it in the 2005 tournament for coming second. In total, Johnny Chan and TJ Cloutier have earned around $3.7m each from the tournament, while Phil Hellmuth Jr has well over $3.5m. However, to achieve these totals, the old pros have all placed in the money dozens of times, unlike some of the 'Johnny-come-latelies' of modern poker.

GAMING IN ART

Some of the world's greatest artists have captured the essence of card play – whether it's joy at winning or sneakily swapping cards behind someone's back. Here are 10 of the best pictures to seek out. The Dutch school of the sixteenth and seventeenth centuries provides a particularly rich hunting ground, as their preference for everyday indoor scenes shows us many images of ordinary folk enjoying a gamble.

Caravaggio
The Cardsharps (c. 1596)
Kimbell Art Museum, Forth Worth

Juan Gris
Glass of Beer and Playing Cards (1913)
Columbus Museum of Art, Ohio

Jacob Duck
Guardroom with Soldiers Playing Cards
(1620-1660)
Museum of Fine Arts, Budapest

William Hogarth
Scene in a Gaming House. (A Rake's Progress). (1732-1734)
Sir John Soane's Museum, London

Jean-Simeon Chardin
The House of Cards (c. 1736-1737)
National Gallery, London

Valentin de Boulogne
Soldiers Playing Cards and Dice (The Cheats) (1620-1622)
National Gallery of Art, Washington

Pieter de Hooch
The Card Players (1663-1665)
Louvre Museum, Paris

Henri de Toulouse Lautrec
The Card Players (1893)
Hahnloser Collection, Switzerland

George Caleb Bingham
Raftsmen Playing Cards (1847)
City Art Museum, St Louis

Hendrick Sorgh
A Woman playing Cards with Two Peasants (1644)
National Gallery, London

CARD SHARP

If scientific reasoning were limited to the logical processes of arithmetic, we should not get very far in our understanding of the physical world. One might as well attempt to grasp the game of poker entirely by the use of the mathematics of probability.
Vannevar Bush, father of the US atomic bomb programme

THE WORLD SERIES OF POKER

The first World Series of Poker, held in 1970 at Binion's Horseshoe in Las Vegas, was won by legendary road gambler Johnny Moss, who took the title by acclamation after winning all five of the events contested. Moss's winnings consisted of a small trophy and whatever money he had managed to take from his fellow gamblers at the table. Since then, the World Series has been contested every year and has attracted a steadily increasing number of entrants – well over 10,000 across its nearly 40 tournaments at last count.

The World Series proper is a broad series of events embracing all the leading forms of poker. But the winner of the Texas hold 'em event is generally regarded as world champion. Here are the winners – and the losers in the final head-to-head – of this biggest of big games since its inception. Players are American unless noted.

YEAR	ENTRANTS	WINNER	PRIZE MONEY
1971	6	Johnny Moss	$30,000
1972	8	Amarillo Slim Preston	$80,000
1973	13	Walter Clyde Pearson	$130,000
1974	16	Johnny Moss	$160,000
1975	21	Brian Roberts	$210,000
1976	22	Doyle Brunson	$220,000
1977	34	Doyle Brunson	$340,000
1978	42	Bobby Baldwin	$210,000
1979	54	Hal Fowler	$270,000
1980	73	Stuey Ungar	$385,000
1981	75	Stuey Ungar	$375,000
1982	104	Jack Straus	$520,000
1983	108	Tom McEvoy	$540,000
1984	132	Jack Keller	$660,000
1985	140	Bill Smith	$700,000
1986	141	Berry Johnston	$570,000
1987	152	Johnny Chan	$655,000
1988	167	Johnny Chan	$700,000
1989	178	Phil Hellmuth Jr	$755,000
1990	194	Mansour Matloubi (Wales)	$895,000
1991	215	Brad Daugherty	$1,000,000

YEAR	ENTRANTS	WINNER	PRIZE MONEY
1992	201	Hamid Dastmalchi	$1,000,000
1993	220	Jim Bechtel	$1,000,000
1994	268	Russ Hamilton	$1,000,000
1995	273	Dan Harrington	$1,000,000
1996	295	Huck Seed	$1,000,000
1997	312	Stuey Ungar	$1,000,000
1998	350	Scotty Nguyen	$1,000,000
1999	393	Noel Furlong (Eire)	$1,000,000
2000	512	Chris Ferguson	$1,500,000
2001	613	Carlos Mortensen (Spain)	$1,500,000
2002	631	Robert Varkonyi	$2,000,000
2003	839	Chris Moneymaker	$2,500,000
2004	2,576	Greg Raymer	$5,000,000
2005	5,619	Joseph Hatchem (Australia)	$7,500,000

POKER PUZZLER

Who is the youngest player to win the WSOP main event?

a) Scott Fischman

b) Phil Hellmuth

c) Julian Gardner

d) Chris Moneymaker

Answer on page 153.

THE HIGH LIFE

Poker's always been associated with mavericks and fast living. In the rarely heard country-swing song 'Take Ma Boots Off When I Die' (sung to the tune of 'There's A Tavern In The Town') Carson Robinson and his Hill Billies lay out the life of a fornicating poker player who 'shot my way from Texas to Rio Grande', but who hopes that 'when they hand me out my wings' he'd be in the clear because he'd taken in the wife and 16 children of a wife-beating killer he's gunned down.

FREEZE OUT

The poker pros who play at *Hustler* publisher Larry Flynt's home game – where millions of dollars change hands over seven-card stud – have learned the hard way about their host's eccentricities. For some unstated reason, Flynt keeps the temperature in his mansion at refrigerator level, forcing his opponents to kit themselves out in thermal underwear to play. One poker ace who neglected the usual precautions was taken to hospital with a mild case of frostbite.

THE BLUFFER'S GUIDE TO BLUFFING

You'll never be a really successful poker player until you master the fine art of bluffing. But where, when and how should you attempt it? Here are some top tips from the pros:

- **It's hard to bluff bad players.** They're the ones who will stay with you, hoping to draw some miracle card. If you know what you're doing, good players can actually be easier to bluff.

- **Stay tight.** Well, tight-ish. If you're renowned as a loose player, your opponents are much more likely to stay with you all the way when you bluff. They won't necessarily have read you – they'll just think you're hoping to draw the miracle cards you need to fill another improbable hand.

- **Exploit weakness.** Your bluff is more likely to succeed against a weak player who has already checked. The ideal time to bluff is in a pot where you're coming in, in a late position and every player before you has checked or folded.

- **Don't try to bluff your way right round a crowded table.** It's much easier to fool one or two players than half a dozen or more. Eventually, someone is bound to call you.

- **Make it look as though you have a shot at a believable strong hand.** Bluffing when the flop implies you might be drawing to a flush or straight is a lot more credible than a huge bet coming out of nowhere.

Rather appropriately, this series of minute differences in card backs with a cherub print are known as 'Fallen Angels'. Each has a slight difference in shading the trained eye can pick out.

TRICKY DICK

Richard Nixon learned to play poker during his service in the US Navy during the Second World War. Although a confirmed Quaker, and thus nominally opposed to gambling, he was taught the principles of the game by fellow officer Jimmy Stewart in 1943. The two men played draw poker and Stewart explained his theory that at draw a player should never stay in the pot unless he was convinced that he was winning at the time of the draw. 'Nixon,' he wrote, 'liked what I said. Soon his playing became tops. He never raised unless he was convinced he had the best hand.' In two months, Nixon won $6,000. 'Nick was,' declared another officer, James Udall, 'as good a poker player as, if not better than, anyone we had ever seen. He played a quiet game, but wasn't afraid of taking chances. He wasn't afraid of running a bluff. Sometimes the stakes were pretty big, but Nick had daring and a flair for knowing what to do.'

CRIMINAL RECORDS

As late as the 1970s, Las Vegas poker was more a criminal activity than it was a sport. So it's no surprise many of its biggest names have had their brushes with the law.

Benny Binion   Fled Texas after being charged with murder.

Amarillo Slim Preston   Pleaded guilty to tax evasion, and in 2003 to three misdemeanour assault charges relating to the abuse of a 12-year-old girl. (Slim nonetheless protests his innocence.)

Johnny Moss   Run out of Vegas for cheating during the 1950s.

Brian 'Sailor' Roberts   Suspect in the murder of drugs kingpin Lee Chagra. (Three soldiers from Fort Brag were eventually convicted of the crime.)

WOMEN OF POKER

Cycalona Gowen

Cycalona 'Clonie' Gowen is one of a new breed of media savvy female poker players. A poised blonde with girl-next-door looks, she is a rising star who's taken full advantage of TV's interest in the subject, and has a popular personal website at www.cloniegowan.com. She's also signed a deal with Full Tilt Poker (www.fulltiltpoker.com) where she plays online regularly.

Clonie first came to world attention when she placed 10th in the World Poker Tour Costa Rica tournament, and then won the televised WPT Ladies Night Invitational, triumphing over the likes of Jennifer Harman and Annie Duke, in 2003. But she had been playing for years before that, driving from her Dallas, Texas, home at the weekend to Shrevesport, Louisiana, and usually returning a few hundred dollars better off.

Caution characterises her game. When she's having bad luck she simply withdraws and goes back to family life. With two children she has always made poker fit around their needs rather than the other way around. Although she hasn't had any gigantic tournament wins she's made money every year and says her longest losing streak has only been a month. As well as securing tournament backing from Full Tilt, Gowen is an active public speaker with a range of corporate clients, and astutely publicises her activities in newspaper and magazine interviews, as well as acting as guest commentator at televised events like the Ultimate Poker Challenge.

VARIETIES OF POKER

Texas Hold 'em

Texas hold 'em – says pro legend Doyle Brunson – is 'the Cadillac of poker'. First played by cowboys on the Texas prairie at the end of the nineteenth century, introduced to Vegas in 1963 by Felton 'Corky' McCorquodale and seen every day played in televised tournaments, the game is easily learned, but deceptively subtle. Each player is dealt two hole cards; after an initial round of betting, three communal cards are dealt which all the players may use to improve their hands. A second betting round follows; then two additional cards are dealt face up, with more betting between each deal. The goal is to make the best possible hand using five of the seven cards available.

CARD SHARP

Poker is... a fascinating, wonderful, intricate adventure on the high seas of human nature.
David A Daniel in *Poker: How to Win at the Great American Game*

LO-HI

The story of 'Treetop' Jack Straus's recovery from an appalling run of luck at the Vegas poker tables back in 1970 has entered gambling legend. Down to his last $40, the celebrated high-roller took the money to the blackjack table and bet every cent of it on a single hand. He won, and continued to wager the whole of his bankroll on each successive deal until he had turned his tiny stake into $500. Returning to his poker game, Straus parlayed the $500 up to $4,000 in a winning session, then boosted his total with another few hours of blackjack. By early afternoon he had worked his bankroll back up to $10,000. He then wagered the entire amount on the Kansas City Chiefs to edge the Superbowl at 2 to 1. The Chiefs won. Jack ended the day with $20,000 in his pocket, back where he needed to be. 'The point,' adds Al Alvarez, telling this story, 'is his refusal to compromise. Each time he bet, he bet all the money he had, from the first $40 to the final $10,000. As Damon Runyon wrote of Sky Masterson, the hero of *Guys and Dolls*, "He will bet all he has, and nobody can bet more than this."'

MONKEY BUSINESS

When in 2005 naturalists discovered a new species of monkey in Bolivia, they decided to auction off the right to name it. They probably anticipated some charitable millionaire or celebrity would buy the right to call it after their favourite football player, their child or even themselves. However the winner of this unusual opportunity was online gaming company Goldenpalace.com, so now the scientific record shows the new species as *Callicebus aureipalatii*. Expect to hear David Attenborough's soothing tones any day now saying: 'And just ahead you can see female Goldenpalace.com monkeys gathered in the trees...'

CARD SHARP

Myself, I am not a good poker player. I drink and smoke and enjoy the game too much. You shouldn't do any of those things if you want to win at poker. Poker is a cold-hearted, deadly game that breaks and bankrupts men. I will caution you that very few fine card-players are the sort of people you or I would like to play with. It's not fun playing against cold-hearted butchers.
Ian Fleming, creator of James Bond

HOW TALL?

Phil Gordon – **6ft 9in**
Jack Straus – **6ft 6in**
Amarillo Slim – **6ft 3in**
(**7ft** including his trademark stetson)
Doyle Brunson – **6ft 3in**
Chris Ferguson – **6ft 1in**
Titanic Thompson – **6ft 0in**
Puggy Pearson – **5ft 9in**
Stuey Ungar – **5ft 4in**
Jennifer Harman – **5ft 2in**

2.30 IN DODGE CITY

Doc Holliday was not only a quick-drawing gambler, he was probably the most famous dentist in the Wild West. Wyatt Earp remembered him as 'The most skilful gambler, and the nerviest, fastest, deadliest man with a six-gun I ever saw.'

His real first names were John Henry, and little John Holliday had a genteel upbringing in the old South, where he caught consumption and trained to be a dentist – not a great combination. He moved to Dallas seeking a drier environment, and there soon realised that his nimble fingers suited a card deck more than a drill. For the next eight years he drifted from state to state, turning up in all those places we're familiar with from too many Westerns – Deadwood, Dodge City, Denver and Cheyenne. By the time he arrived in Tombstone, Arizona, in 1880, he already had a formidable reputation as a poker player and killer – cemented by his involvement in the gunfight at the OK Corral where he joined his friend Wyatt Earp and Earp's brothers in a standoff with the Clanton Gang, a band of ruffians who'd been terrorising the town.

People's desire to say they'd sat down to cards with the infamous Doc Holliday obviously overcame their nervousness at being shot, or he'd never have found any partners. He drifted on afterwards and died in 1887 in Glenwood Springs, Colorado, where he'd gone seeking a cure for his TB at the sulphur springs. According to contemporary storytellers, after falling into a state of delirium for several days, the legend has it he woke up suddenly lucid, drank a glass of whiskey, said 'This is funny,' and dropped dead.

MARVELLOUS MR MOSS

Once upon a time poker players stayed at the table until someone walked off with a huge pile of cash. Johnny Moss was raised to play the game like that, and in common with most of the old professionals he was a tough old bird, able to exist on tiny amounts of sleep and to keep his concentration during play that went on day into night into day. Once, after playing for several days straight, he suffered a heart attack and was taken off to hospital. His opponents played on, thinking that was the last they'd seen of him, but later the same day he appeared again at the table, to everyone's amazement. Moss took their surprise in good part. "It was only a mild heart attack," he explained.

POKER PROSE

Kitty 'The Schemer' LeRoy arrived in Deadwood on the same wagon train as 'Wild Bill' Hickok, Colorado Charlie Utter and Calamity Jane, in July 1876. For a few years, her gambling and bragging made her the queen of Deadwood's colourful underworld, until her unique way with men led to her downfall...

Her physical appearance aside, it was generally agreed that Kitty was a clever gambler. 'A good player... inordinately fond of money,' conceded a Deadwood townsman; 'a terrific gambler,' gushed a bemused newsman. 'Kitty was sometimes rich and sometimes poor, but always lavish as a prince when she had some money,' said the reporter. 'She dealt... faro, and played all games and cards with a dexterity that amounted to genius.'
To say that Kitty LeRoy was flamboyant would be an understatement. According to the hyperbolic journalist, she dressed like a gypsy, 'had five husbands, seven revolvers, a dozen bowie-knives and always went armed to the teeth... She could throw a bowie knife straighter than any pistol bullet, except her own.' It was said that more men had been killed in fights over Kitty than over all the other women in town combined.

She could do her own fighting when the occasion demanded. Once she donned masculine clothing to challenge a fellow who refused to fight a woman. She gunned him down and then, suddenly contrite, called for a preacher and married her victim before he died. She claimed to have chosen her first husband from an assortment of suitors because he was the only one with nerve enough to let her shoot an apple off his head as she rode her horse past at a full gallop.

Another husband was a German prospector who had made a modestly successful strike in the Black Hills. She got $8,000 in gold from the German, but when his claim played out, broke a bottle over his head and kicked him out the door.

Kitty the Schemer was 28 when her remarkable career came to an abrupt, violent end in Deadwood. Her fifth husband, a man named Sam Curley, balked when she tired of him and showed him the door. He pulled a .45, blew a large hole in Kitty, then turned the gun on himself.

Robert K DeArment, *Knights of the Green Cloth: The Saga of Frontier Gamblers* (1982)

COME RIGHT ON IN

Not that we want to put you off or anything, but here are
some casinos that sound less than welcoming...

1. **Hard Rock** – designed to put you between one and a hard place, financially

2. **Mirage** – never was a truer name coined for the glitz and glamour of gambling

3. **Hotel California** – fans of the Eagles song might not be so taken with the name

4. **Casino Royale** – fans of the James Bond film may well recall the casino carnage scene...

5. **Sahara** – a big expanse of nothingness, but at least at this one you get free drinks

6. **Boulder Station** – rocks aren't exactly romantic or sexy, even big ones

7. **Terrible's** – need we say more?

POKER PUZZLER

Which of the following was the first online poker room?
a) Play Poker
b) Planet Poker
c) The Poker Place
d) 888
Answer on page 153.

MISSIONARY IMPOSSIBLE

In a season 11 episode of *The Simpsons* from 2000, Homer becomes a missionary in the South Pacific having begged Reverend Lovejoy's help in escaping from 'enforcers' from PBS television, to whom he's pledged $10,000 to save his favourite sitcom. With Mr Rogers, the Teletubbies and Oscar the Grouch on his tail, he jumps inside a sack labelled 'Children's letters to God' and winds up on a tropical island, trying to teach the natives the values of Christianity. Being Homer, of course, he builds the 'Lucky Savage' casino and swiftly introduces them to the joys of gambling and beer drinking instead.

FIT FOR OFFICE

Asked by censorious newsmen to comment on his former pupil Richard Nixon's poker-playing habits, Dr Albert Upton of Whittier College, California, replied: 'A man who couldn't hold a hand in a first-class poker game is not fit to be President of the United States.'

Don't let poker come between you and the missus – teach her to play, too!

INTUITION

What made Stuey Ungar one of the great poker players of all time? His unmatched card sense? His unrelenting aggression? Perhaps. But many card gurus believe the most astonishing of all Ungar's talents was his uncanny ability to read opponents.

Phil Hellmuth illustrates the point with a story about Ungar's disastrous 1990 World Series of Poker. With one day to go, Stuey was a strong favourite to go through to the final table. That night, though, he 'fell ill' (translation: OD'd on crack cocaine) and took no part in the last day's play. Cardiff's Mansour Matloubi was champion that year.

When Ungar recovered, he challenged Matloubi to play a heads-up, no-limit freeze-out, both men putting up $50,000. Mansour accepted the challenge, and the two men were roughly level after 45 minutes' play when the champ called Ungar's opening blind with a dreadful hand, 4-5 offsuit. The flop came 3-3-7 and Stuey bet $6,000. Mansour now had a sniff at a straight, and he called again, but the turn and the river brought only K-Q. Matloubi, sensing weakness in Ungar's hand, nonetheless went all in, betting $32,000. Stuey, Hellmuth recalls, looked 'right through'

his opponent. Then he said: 'You have 4-5 or 5-6. I'm gonna call you with this,' flipping the truly appalling hand 10-9.

'Wow!' Hellmuth wrote. 'What an unbelievable call! Stuey can't even beat a jack-high bluff with his hand, never mind any pair. In fact, Stuey could only beat 4-5, 4-6 or 5-6 in this scenario. Give Mansour some credit. He did read Stuey right and made a great bluff. But Stuey deserves even more credit. He not only read Mansour right, he then made an amazing call.'

Few pros would risk losing a freeze-out playing a 10-high hand. But Ungar was so sure he knew his opponent's cards that he called without hesitation. Matloubi simply did not believe it. He looked, Hellmuth recalled, 'like a bulldozer just ran over him'.

Ungar's opponent was world champ, but the experience still shook him to the core. 'When a guy makes a call like that,' he told Hellmuth, 'you just give up. It's like he's taken all the wind out of your sails. I decided I couldn't play any more heads-up no-limit hold 'em, at least on that day, if not forever.' And, indeed, the hand did prove to be the last the two men ever played together.

NOT TOO MUCH OF A FLUTTER

If you're in Las Vegas and fancy a gamble, but not too much of a gamble mind, here are the best casinos in which to find Texas hold 'em tables for low-stakes players:

Aladdin · Bally's · Cannery
Excalibur · Flamingo · Gold Coast
Golden Nugget · Harrah's
Imperial Palace · Jokers Wild
Luxor · MGM Grand · Monte Carlo
Orleans · Palace Station · Palms
Plaza · Riviera · Sahara
Sam's Town · Speedway
Stratosphere · Tropicana

HALL OF FAME

The Poker Hall of Fame has always recognised players' players, consistently strong gamblers who may not have won all the major titles, but who became familiar faces in Vegas.

1991 – David 'Chip' Reese
Reese started playing poker at the age of 6, and hit Las Vegas in 1974 with $400 in his pocket, planning to stay the weekend and play a little poker. That same weekend he won $60,000 in a poker tournament and never left.

1992 – 'Amarillo Slim' Preston
An outrageous character, famous for his books, his side bets and for winning many major tournaments, including the World Series in 1972, Slim now lives in semi-retirement in his native Texas, having survived games with Richard Nixon and Pablo Escobar.

1993 – 'Gentleman' Jack Keller
When Keller left the Air Force in the early 1980s, he headed straight for Vegas, and by 1984 had claimed the World Series title. For two decades he was a fixture of the poker world, playing a terrifyingly consistent game.

CARD SHARP

POKER, *n.* *A game said to be played with cards for some purpose to this lexicographer unknown.*
Ambrose Bierce, US journalist, short-story writer, *The Devil's Dictionary* (1911)

BEST POKER MOVIES

Sometimes memorable poker scenes are used to kick off a film, to set up the dramatic tension that will fuel the action. And sometimes they're the entire focus.

Lock, Stock and Two Smoking Barrels (1998)

1998 was the year for poker movies. Hugely popular British gangster flick starts with four ordinary joes who club together to fund a friend in a high-stakes game against a local London gangster. When they lose they're forced into crime to try and meet the debt.

Big Deal In Dodge City (1966)

(known as *A Big Hand for the Little Lady* in the US)
Benign comedy Western in which Henry Fonda moves his family to a new town and promptly gets in over his head in a poker game and bets his life savings. He has a heart attack, leaving his wife, played by Joanna Woodward, to take his place in the game, despite the fact she's never played poker before.

Loaded Pistols (1948)

Classic Western in which a young man is accused of committing murder during a poker game, when all the lights suddenly go out. His sister, played by Barbara Britton, enlists Gene Autry to help hide him, and solve the murder. Autry recreates the game and is able to prove who really did it.

Sunset Trail (1939)

William Boyd stars as Hopalong Cassidy, out to revenge a poor farmer who's been killed in a crooked cattle deal. With the help of his daughter, Cassidy poses as a novice poker player to entrap the bad guys.

Titanic (1997)

Leonardo di Caprio wins the fateful tickets for a passage on the *Titanic* in a poker game at the start of the film. Director James Cameron knew nothing about poker and had someone else set up the scene for him – some wags will say that this isn't a surprise given that the game was unlikely to be played by Irish peasants in 1912!

THE GAMBLER

Few Country and Western songs get turned into films... and few Country and Western stars get to play the hero in the film of their song. So luck was obviously with Kenny Rogers when he wrote: 'You've got to know when to hold 'em, know when to fold 'em...' Of course, many people who've seen some of *The Gambler* films may say 'Amen to that'. If you're one of the people who's failed to thrill to Mr Rogers' acting talent, you may be surprised to hear that they made not one, but four, sequels.

Kenny Rogers as *The Gambler* (1980)
Original (and I'm afraid best) of a bad bunch, with spade-bearded Kenny Rogers as loveable rogue Brady Hawkes, Bruce Boxleitner as his cocky sidekick Billy Montana, and Linda Evans as fiery love interest Kate Muldoon. Hawkes gets a letter from his son, who's in trouble, and sets off to the rescue.

Kenny Rogers as *The Gambler: The Adventure Continues* (1983)
Now joined by his son Jeremiah, Hawkes and pals are on a train to a big poker tournament when it's held up by a bunch of desperados who take Jeremiah hostage. It's Daddy to the rescue once more.

Kenny Rogers as *The Gambler: The Legend Continues* (1987)
Hawkes and Montana are back, teaming up with a bunch of Sioux who're being diddled by corrupt government officials. No Linda Evans, but there are some great character names like Sgt Grinder and Charles Afraid of Bear.

The Gambler Returns: The Luck of the Draw (1991)
What's more horrifying than outlaws, gunmen and wild 'injuns'? Why, a law to outlaw gambling. As a last hurrah, America's greatest gamblers are gathering in San Francisco for a game to beat all games, with a $100,000 entrance fee. Hawkes, backed by a quintet of madams led by Reba McEntire, sets out to win, but will he live to reach San Francisco, let alone play? Take a guess.

The Gambler V: Playing for Keeps (1994)
Young Jeremiah has grown up and become tangled up with Butch Cassidy and the Sundance Kid (previous films featured just about every other well-known Western character, so this is no surprise to fans). Daddy to the rescue yet again...

(Not only did Kenny Rogers turn one song into a five-film franchise, he also appeared in *Coward of the County*, based on yet another of his songs. More a singing R&D department than a musician, one feels.)

'SPACE AT TABLE 243!'

There are few things more annoying than turning up at a casino, ready to play, only to find every seat taken and the card room jammed. Next time it happens to you, try one of these fine institutions:

The Commerce, *Los Angeles*	**200 tables**
The Bicycle Club, *Los Angeles*	**180 tables**
Inglewood Casino, *Los Angeles*	**150 tables**
Trump Taj Mahal, *Atlantic City*	**68 tables**
Bellagio Hotel, *Las Vegas*	**40 tables**
Borgata, *Atlantic City*	**34 tables**
Mirage, *Las Vegas*	**31 tables**
Wynn Casino, *Las Vegas*	**27 tables**
Orleans, *Las Vegas*	**23 tables**
MGM Grand, *Las Vegas*	**23 tables**
Grand Casino Biloxi, *Mississippi*	**21 tables**
Excalibur, *Las Vegas*	**20 tables**
Binion's Horseshoe, *Las Vegas*	**18 tables**

VARIETIES OF POKER

Stud Poker

Stud poker, a cowboy favourite, appeared in the second half of the nineteenth century and was the main game, other than draw poker, dealt until the 1960s. It can be played with either five or seven cards, but the general principle remains the same: four of each player's cards are dealt face up, one by one, with betting rounds between each deal, and the remainder (either one card or three) face down, improving the vital element of bluff.

Nowadays five-card stud is practically extinct, having vanished around 1980 with the retirement of Bill Boyd, a master player so brilliant that in the end he could find no one to play the game against him. The more complex and action-packed seven-card variety is still widely played today, however, and is the favourite game of publishing magnate Larry Flynt.

POKER PROSE

During the 1870s, before straights and flushes were introduced to poker, there were two hands guaranteed to win any pot: four aces, or four kings and an ace. When either appeared, it was greeted with the same reverence players now accord to an ace-high straight flush, as this famous story of the period explains.

One morning the janitor of a Denver bank opened the door and was surprised to observe three rather tired-looking citizens seated on the steps, the centre one of whom held a sealed envelope carefully in sight of his companions.

'Want to make a deposit, gentlemen?' asked the cashier, who shortly arrived. 'Step inside.'

'No, I want to negotiate a loan,' said the man with the envelope, 'and there ain't a moment to lose. I want $5,000 quicker than hell can scorch a feather.'

'What collaterals have you – Government bonds?' inquired the bank official.

'Government nothin'. I've got something that beats four per cents all hollow. You see, I've been sitting in a poker game across the street, and there's over $4,000 in the pot. There are three or four pretty strong hands out, and as I've every cent in the centre the boys have given me thirty minutes to raise a stake on my hand. It's in this envelope. Just look at it, but don't give it away to these gentlemen. They're in the game, and came along to see I don't monkey with the cards.'

'But, my dear sir,' said the cashier, who had quietly opened the envelope and found it to contain four kings and an ace. 'This is certainly irregular – we don't lend money on cards.'

'But you ain't going to see me raised out on a hand like that,' whispered the pokerist. 'These fellows think I'm bluffing and I can just clean out the whole gang.'

'Can't help it, sir. Never heard of such a thing,' said the cashier, and the disappointed applicant and his friends drifted sadly out. On the corner they met the bank's president, who was himself just from a quiet little all-night game. They explained the case again, and the next moment the superior officer darted into the bank, seized a bag of twenties, and an extra handful of twenties, which he flung on the counter.

'Why, I thought you had more business snap,' the president said to the cashier. 'Ever play poker?'

'No, sir.'

'Ah, thought not – thought not. If you did, you'd know what good collateral was. Remember that in future four kings and an ace are always good in this institution for our entire assets, sir – our entire assets.'

John Lillard, *Poker Stories As Told By Statesmen, Soldiers, Lawyers, Commercial Travelers, Bankers, Actors, Editors, Millionaires, Members of the Ananias Club and the Talent, Embracing the Most Remarkable Games 1845-95* (1896)

Man: 'This tennis is awfully boring... I suppose a quick
hand of strip poker's out of the question, ladies?'

THE POKER WALK OF FAME

A new tourist attraction, based on the famous Hollywood Walk of Fame on Hollywood Boulevard, opened at the Commerce Casino in California – home of the world's largest poker room – in 2004.

Organised by the World Poker Tour in direct competition with the Horseshoe casino's Poker Hall of Fame, the new Poker Walk of Fame can't compete with the Hollywood version just yet – so far it boasts only three stars to LA's 2,130. But maybe it will get there in time.

The three inaugural inductees were poker doyen Doyle Brunson, Gus 'The Great Dane' Hanson, widely regarded as the best young player in the world, and actor James Garner, who popularised the game by starring in the 1960s TV Western, *Maverick*.

CARD SHARP

This must be my lucky day.
'Wild Bill' Hickok, on receiving the poker hand that he
was holding when he was shot dead

WOMEN OF POKER

Alice Ivers

One of the most celebrated female poker players in the old West was Alice Ivers, better known as 'Poker Alice'. Throughout her life, Alice turned to poker when she was bereaved. Widowed by her first American husband, a mining engineer named Frank Duffield, in Colorado, she began to hang out in the city's gambling halls and learned how to deal poker professionally.

Alice is chiefly remembered for her youthful presence in Deadwood when the camp was just being established. In her early 20s, Alice was beautiful and ballsy, by turns gambler, bootlegger and brothel madam. As a woman doing an unusual job, she attracted aggressive men who thought they could beat her, and she always carried a .38, which she wasn't afraid to use. Although most of her play was steady (steady enough to support a husband and family) she would sometimes throw caution to the wind and take on all comers. She also went on wild spending sprees, bringing back trunks of beautiful clothes from New York.

Her second husband was also a gambler, Warren G Tubbs, but not a very good one. He took up painting instead, leaving the cards to her, as she regularly beat him. When Tubbs died from TB, acquired while he was painting, Alice left Deadwood and, now in her late 50s, gamed her way through Rapid City to Sturgis, South Dakota. There she met and married her third husband, George Huckert, but it didn't last long. By now Alice was tiring of her fast-paced life. Instead of her beautiful clothes, she took to wearing a man's shirt and a battered hat, and won less and less as gambling lost its charm and began to bore her. She bootlegged alcohol until the arrival of Prohibition, and then ran a brothel in Sturgis, occasionally returning to dealing poker at big city saloons, where people still remembered her name. She died in 1930, at the age of 77, a relic of a wild, rough period in the history of the West.

POKER MAXIMS TO LIVE BY

- 'Trust everyone,' legendary casino owner Benny Binion used to say, 'but always shuffle the cards.'

- 'I wouldn't pay a 10-year-old kid a dime an hour to sit in a low-stakes game and wait for the nuts,' poker purist Jack Straus famously said. 'If there's no risk in losing, there's no high in winning. I have only a limited amount of time on this earth and I want to live every second of it. That's why I'm willing to play any-one in the world for any amount. It doesn't matter who they are. They all look like dragons to me, and I want to slay them.'

- 'Poker,' wrote Somerset Maugham in *Cosmopolitans*, 'is the only game fit for a grown man. Then, your hand is against every man's, and every man's hand is against yours. Teamwork? Whoever made a fortune by teamwork? There's only one way to make a fortune, and that's to down the fellow who's up against you.'

SIGN OF THE TIMES

In America, revenues from gambling run in inverse proportion to the American econ-omy. When the economy is doing badly, state legislature tends to favour gambling because the building of casinos, racetracks and creation of lotteries brings in much-needed revenue and helps jumpstart local economies.

In the 1980s, gambling revenue went up sharply thanks to freehanded legislation, only slowing in the late 1990s as the American economy improved – mind you, in 1997, overall revenues still rose by 14% year on year, so it wasn't exactly stalled.

Casinos were the hardest hit, if you can call it that. In 1996, casino revenues stood at $20.9bn, and in 1997, they rose to $22bn, an increase of around 5%. This was dramatic because in the early 1990s, a lot of new markets had been opened up and a lot of new casinos opened. With the economy sluggish again, the huge interest in poker is pushing up gaming revenues once again, chiefly through online sites.

THE BIG FIXER

Professional gambler Arnold Rothstein, known as 'Mr Big', was one of the most colourful characters in gambling in the first two decades of the last century – and one of the most infamous. Supposedly the inspiration for both Truman Capote's Nathan Detroit in *Guys and Dolls* and F Scott Fitzgerald's Meyer Wolfsheim in *The Great Gatsby*, Rothstein is rumoured to be the man who fixed the 1919 World Series of Baseball.

He began life as a cigar salesman, saved hard, and when he had $2,000 in his pocket began gambling professionally, shooting craps, playing pool and poker, his philosophy: 'If a man is dumb, someone is going to get the best of him, so why not you? If you don't, you're as dumb as he is.'

By 1914, Rothstein was notorious in New York, where he ran a successful gambling house and had revolutionised the bookkeeping business by organising a lot of independent operators into a single money-making operation. With this funding, he became known as the man who could fund any lay-off bet, no matter how huge, a practice that continued until his death. But history will remember him for the huge bets he placed. In 1921, he won $850,000 on his own horse, Sidereal, in an Independence Day race, and only a few weeks later, won a further $500,000 on another of his horses, Sporting Blood, in the Travers Stakes.

Even Rothstein's death was infamous. He was shot in the Park Central Hotel, New York, which housed one of the city's biggest gambling dens, on 4 November 1928. He'd been asked to go to the hotel by George McManus, another gambler, who met him in room 349 and shot him. Both had taken part in a marathon poker game that started on 8 September and went on until 10 September. Rothstein had left owing huge sums to his fellow players without even giving them an IOU for his losses: he owed over $300,000 to Nate Raymond, Joe Bernstein and 'Titanic' Thompson. This was normal practice for him, and they expected him to make good on his debts swiftly, but days then weeks passed and nothing was forthcoming.

Rothstein staggered down the service stairs and tried to get a cab to take him home. He died two days later on Election Day. As was his wont, he'd bet heavily on the outcome, and would have pocketed $570,000.

POKER PUZZLER

Which of the following players have gone on record as having helped Ben Affleck learn how to play better poker – pick as many answers as you like.

a) Phil Hellmuth
b) Jennifer Harman
c) Antonio Esfandiari
d) Johnny Chan
e) TJ Cloutier
f) Annie Duke
g) Chris Ferguson
h) Tom McEvoy

Answer on page 153.

IF ONLY THEY PLAYED

The website 888.com recently asked gambling expert Mark Griffiths to assess which prominent public figures would do well if they decided to take up poker... and which should give up even thinking about it.

Great Potential (people who display skill at problem solving, are strategic thinkers, self controlled, practical and numerate):
Chancellor of the Exchequer Gordon Brown
Playwright and comic Ben Elton
Glamour model Jordan
Presenter Davina McCall
Arsenal Manager Arsene Wenger
Former England Rugby Coach Sir Clive Woodward

Stinkers:
England Football captain David Beckham
Prime Minister Tony Blair
Politician David Blunkett
Footballer Ashley Cole
Footballer Rio Ferdinand

ON EDGE

Ways to keep those around you off kilter before they even think about looking at their first cards.

Dress for Sex
Only really useful for female players. But they can really use their looks, vulnerability and cleavage to manipulate other gamblers.

All that Scratching
Not only is scratching catching – watch someone scratch and you'll start finding your own overpowering itches – but the noise of it (particularly long nails on nylon tights, ladies) can drive listeners crazy and send shivers up the spine.

Habit Forming
Teeth grinding, clicking, finger tapping and snapping, leg swinging and twitching are all great distractions – so long as they don't form part of your tell. Someone who wriggles and shifts a lot makes everyone else feel uncomfortable too.

Health Scares
Poker's a stressful game and it's not unknown for people to keel over under all that pressure. Spasms, chest pains and other easily faked symptoms could put your opponents off a good deal more than you – since you've planned them in advance.

STRINGING YOU ALONG

'In a Western,' poker writer Lou Krieger observes, 'someone's always saying: "Mighty big bet, cowboy. I'll just see your 20," while reaching back into his stack for more chips, and with a long, lingering glance for effect, drawling, "…and raise you 40!"' Try that in real life, though, and at least one of the players at your table is likely to object with a shout of 'String raise!' or 'String bet!' Calling a bet, and then attempting a raise, is illegal in poker because it gives a player the chance to gauge his opponents' reactions before he commits a lot of chips. Still, there's one thing worse than the embarrassment of being called on a string bet. Says Krieger: 'Now, if someone shouts, "String raise!" and another opponent says something like, "That's OK. Let his raise stand," be assured your hand is in big trouble. Real big trouble.'

CARD SHARP

*The next best thing to playing and winning is playing
and losing. The main thing is to play.*
Nick 'The Greek' Dandalos, in *Gambling Secrets of Nick the Greek*

POKER MUSEUMS

Want to bone up on the history of the game? Much poker information is tied up in more general collections of playing cards and gaming books. But if you're willing to search you can certainly profit from your learning. Here's some destinations for the poker tourist:

Nevada Museum of Gambling,
Virginia City, Nevada, USA
Exemplary displays of methods of cheating – to warn you before you get to Vegas.

**Frederic Jessel Collection,
Bodleian Library**, *Oxford, England*
Has 3,500 items relating to the history and use of cards and card games. Accessible only to members of the library. Readers' tickets may be obtained from the Admissions Office, Clarendon Building, Broad Street.
T: +44 (0)1865 277179 / 277180.

Elliott Avedon Museum and Archive of Games, *University of Waterloo, Ontario, Canada*
Covers all games, not just cards, with fascinating stuff about the geographical spread of games and origins of playing cards.

Beinecke Rare Book and Manuscript Library, *Yale University, New Haven, USA*
Has 1,000 different packs of cards and related books on gaming, stretching back 500 years.

Deutsches Spielkartenmuseum,
Leinfelden-Echterdingen, near Stuttgart, Germany
German playing card museum with poker cards.

Baoguo Temple, *Ningbo, China*
The Baoguo Temple has thousands of sets of poker cards on display – there are over 150,000 playing card collectors in China alone.

Musée Francais de la carte à jouer,
Issy-les-Moulineaux, near Paris, France
'France's only playing card museum' is their slogan. You don't say...

139

POKER PUZZLER

In cockney rhyming slang, to gamble is to:

a) *Go for a ramble* (obvious, but also a reference to the
pointlessness of the exercise, ie you'll never win)
b) *Have a Glen* (Campbell, from the country singer)
c) *Have a Sol* (Campbell, from the popular footballer)
d) *Get your feet wet* (from have a bet)
Answer on page 153.

PLAIN BROWN WRAPPER

'Treetop' Jack Straus, the much-beloved 6ft 7in poker giant, was renowned for gambling every dollar he possessed. He carried his bankroll around with him, thousands of dollars casually stuffed into a brown paper bag. On more than one occasion, Straus mislaid the bag and wound up flat broke.

POKER – A SIGHT FOR SORE EYES?

Everyone says staying up all night, sitting for hours in a smoky atmosphere, and everything else associated with the poker player's lifestyle is harmful to the human body, but Johnny Moss wouldn't agree with them. 'Listen here,' he told journalist Chris Calhoun. 'A couple of years ago I bent down to tie my shoe and my glasses dropped off. I'd been wearing bifocals for 25 years and now I can see my shoes better without 'em. Well, I go to the eye doctor and I read that whole damned chart. I got 20-20 vision again. Lookee here, see what I'm sayin'?' He then showed Calhoun his driver's licence with 'No restrictions' on it.

Moss revealed that he tilted back and forward in his chair throughout games to keep the blood flowing, repeating the motion thousands of times, and that in other games he would catnap between rounds, getting a few minutes sleep here and there. The person next to him would give him a nudge when it was his turn to play. I'm sure many of the people he beat would be just delighted to know he did it while half asleep.

TELL IT AS IT IS

Most players, says tells guru Mike Caro, display signs of nervousness only when they're actually in little danger. Those playing weak hands or attempting to bluff are sufficiently conscious of the dangers to make every effort to conceal their worry. One of the best ways of catching an opponent bluffing is to watch for the cessation of any nervous ticks, such as twitching of legs under the table. Conversely, there are fear players who tremble when they bet. It's not fear that causes them to shake – it's the release of tension once a decision is made.

SPORTING SHOWDOWN

Just as several notable poker professionals also shine at other sports, many sportspeople are also very keen card players. Here are some who enjoy a tussle over the tables:

Alan Brazil – ex footballer and Talksport radio presenter
Steve Davis – snooker player and prog rock fancier
Jeff Gordon – NASCAR champion driver
Tony Hawk – the world's best-known skateboarder
Stephen Hendry – snooker player
Paul Ince – first black England football captain, currently captain of West Ham
John McCririck – racing commentator
Dennis Rodman – outrageous basketball star
Teddy Sheringham – footballer
Jimmy White – snooker player

KNOW YOUR OPPOSITION

Poker is a game of skill, not chance. But that's not to say the cards you're dealt dictate your success. Probably the most vital talent you can have is the ability to take the best advantage of your opponent's mistakes. 'Most of the money you'll win at poker comes not from the brilliance of your own play,' veterans Richard Harroch and Lou Krieger say, 'but from the ineptitude of your opponents.'

WHERE'S THE TOURNAMENT?

When and where to find tournaments to join in Las Vegas – anyone can take part so long as they put up the fee, and you could find yourself sitting down at a table in a famous casino like the Bellagio that's just been vacated by one of the most famous poker players in the world.

Aladdin (Monday-Friday)
Bellagio (daily)
Binion's (daily)
Cannery (daily)
Circus Circus (Monday-Friday)
Club Fortune (daily)
Flamingo (Monday-Friday)
Golden Nugget (daily)
Harrah's (daily)
Imperial Palace (Sunday-Thursday)
Jokers Wild (daily)
Luxor (daily)
Mandalay Bay (Monday-Friday)
Mirage (Sunday-Thursday)
Nevada Palace (daily)
Orleans (daily)
Plaza (daily)
Poker Palace (Saturday)
Rio (daily)
Sahara (daily)
Sam's Town (Friday-Sunday)
Stardust (Monday-Wednesday)
Stratosphere (Monday-Friday)
Sunset Station (daily)
Texas Station (Tuesday)

CARD SHARP

Never play cards with a man named Doc, and never eat at a place called Mom's.
Nelson Algren, writer

SMART COOKIE

Crandall Addington, a wealthy Texas oilman and real-estate magnate, was the fashion plate of the World Series of Poker in its early days. Twice runner-up at the final table, Addington was best known for his neatly trimmed beard, mink Stetson, silk shirts and exquisite linen suits. But those who underestimated his abilities at the table did so at their peril. Although always an amateur player, Addington is remembered for some classic advice on playing no-limit Texas hold 'em. 'A friend,' writes Al Alvarez, who overheard the conversation, 'had been dealt a 10 of hearts and had called a raise from someone sitting in an early position. The flop was a black king and two low hearts, a six and a deuce; there was $2,000 in the pot. An early raise before the flop usually indicates a player is holding an ace and a king. Sure enough, the man came out betting.

'"How much?" Addington asked.

'"The pot," said the friend. "Two thousand dollars."

'"So what did you do?"

'"I just flat called him."

'"Wrong," said Addington. "You should have raised him $15,000 and let him think about it."

WOMEN OF POKER

Wendeen Eolis

Unlike most of her fellow poker pros, Wendeen Eolis didn't even start playing poker until she was 40, in 1984. She went on to become the first woman ever to place in the money in the World Series of Poker, an event which was commemorated by Binion's Horseshoe casino when they issued a commemorative chip with her likeness on it.

She also remains the only woman to win the European Open No-Limit event, and has set no less than seven records for a female poker player, all the time holding down a regular day job as a senior gubernatorial adviser and later as CEO of her own company.

Eolis is a true pioneer, a mistress of no-limit hold 'em who has never sacrificed her femininity to play poker. Indeed it's well known that if she had her way she would introduce new rules to bring a stricter code of gentlemanly conduct to the world's poker rooms. First lady of poker indeed.

Make sure you have a good grasp of scoring before starting a game. Long delays and head scratching will soon mark you out as a newcomer ripe for the plucking.

HEAVY WEIGHT

To commemorate the silver anniversary of the World Series of Poker, 1994 champ Russ Hamilton received his own weight in silver in addition to the usual $1m prize money. Unluckily for the organisers, the podgy Hamilton weighed in at 330lb and scooped silver bars valued at an additional $28,512.

VARIETIES OF POKER

Seven-Card Stud Eight-or-Better

Seven-card stud eight-or-better is one of the hi-lo split games gaining in popularity at present. A fairly recent modification of the old seven-card stud hi-lo, it requires a player to have five unpaired cards ranked 8 or lower in their hand to stake a claim on the low pot. Aces can be either high or low.

POKER HOLIDAYS

Amarillo Slim claims to have come up with the idea of poker cruises years ago and for several years companies have quietly been running them, often using them to attract tourists during the low season. But it was not until the recent poker craze that they really started to take off in a big way. The idea is simple. You go on a boat round some exotic, attractive foreign places, and ignore them all while playing poker all day and most of the night. Only kidding. As the brochures are quick to point out, poker's kind of an anti-social game, with long hours spend in semi-dark rooms, no fun or sunshine, so here's your opportunity to combine it with something a bit more healthy, something a bit more sociable, something that will expand your mind and, who knows, maybe even find you a girlfriend or boyfriend.

The cruises are also useful for poker widows/widowers – they know there's a whole programme of activities and sights to see while their loved ones are hunched over the tables. Some cruises even go so far as to only open the poker room when the ship is at sea and most run a variety of tournaments on board with buy-ins under the £100 mark. Most are run from the west coast of America, and prices start around £450, although that doesn't include flights to the States.

Usually the boats are regular cruise boats with their own casinos featuring such games as roulette, blackjack and lots and lots of slots. But on a poker cruise the slots stay silent and everything focuses on the poker room – sometimes a conference room or two that's been turned over for the duration if there's no room in the regular casino.

Of course, if you get seasick there are also Poker Fantasy Camps, where professionals and keen amateurs mix, and the latter pick up tips, hone their skills with their idols, and play each other in tournaments. Camps aren't the cheap option, however. This year, three nights at a Vegas casino attending Howard 'The Professor' Lederer's Fantasy Camp cost about £1,700, excluding travel. For that money you'll get to play in two hold 'em tournaments, you'll get to sit across from a couple of the world's best players, you'll get all the buffets you can waddle past and the chance to attend lectures on the esoterica of poker playing.

And, ultimately, you can lose that sort of money in a game in a few minutes, so if you look at it like that, it's amazing value.

For more information check out:
www.cardplayercruises.com
www.classicpokercruises.com
www.allincamp.com

CARD SHARP

Last night I stayed up late playing poker with Tarot cards.
I got a full house and four people died.
Steven Wright, comedian

POKER PROSE

Fortunes were made and lost on the turn of a card on the Mississippi river boats.
Gamblers, professional or otherwise, could lose tens of thousands of pounds in a few
minutes. The story of John Powell, illustrates the ups and downs of the gambler's life.

Perhaps the most dashing and romantic of the river-boat gamblers was John Powell, a tall, handsome, well-educated Missourian whose personal charm made him an intimate of the most affluent and influential men of the South. He was a welcome visitor in the finest homes along the river. A close friend of Andrew Jackson and Stephen A Douglas, Powell was offered a nomination for a seat in Congress but refused.

John Powell was conceded by his peers to be one of the cleverest poker players in the South. After taking to the river in 1845, he enjoyed great success for some thirteen years. In the year 1858 he participated in a memorable poker game aboard the steamer *Atlantic*, involving two other professionals and a wealthy planter named Devereaux. When the game broke up after three days and nights of continuous play, the four players owed a bar bill of $791.50, Devereaux was $100,000 poorer, and Powell had pocketed something in excess of $50,000. Shortly after this extraordinary game, Powell relieved a young English traveler of his $8,000 bankroll and all of his luggage. The distraught Englishman went to his stateroom and shot himself in the head. Learning of the suicide, Powell was shattered with guilt. Sending the money and baggage to the young man's family in England, he retired from gambling for a year. He was 50 years old at this time and financially well off. He owned a theatre and other real estate in New Orleans, a farm worth $100,000 in Tennessee and a number of properties in Saint Louis. Still he could not resist the lure of the river-boat gambling tables. He returned to the old life, but some part of his former skill and boldness was gone. Within a year he had lost his entire fortune. He went to Seattle during the Civil War and died there, a pauper, in 1870.

Robert K DeArment, *Knights of the Green Cloth:*
The Saga of the Frontier Gamblers (1982)

MEMORABLE POKER SCENES

Whether it's the intensity or the sheer strangeness of it all, here are six poker moments on the silver screen that you'll not want to miss:

1. *Run* (1990)

Fine evocation of illegal gaming in New Jersey. Patrick Dempsey plays a guy marking time at a smoky, edgy game, which ends with a showdown where another angry player forces him to draw a card he doesn't want. A little gem.

2. *The Sting* (1973)

The on-train poker game where a half drunk, nasty Newman out-cheats Robert Shaw while allowing him to believe he's the one doing the hustling.

3. *California Split* (1974)

Robert Altman's great forgotten poker movie staring Altman regulars George Segal and Elliot Gould as two gamblers who spend their days moving from the track to the casino in search of a fix.

4. *Born Yesterday* (1950)

Forget the Don Johnson/Melanie Griffith remake. Judy Holliday as a dumb or not-so-dumb blonde playing gin and Broderick Crawford as the debased man who keeps her.

5. *Dr Mabuse – The Gambler* (1922)

German Expressionist sequel (not a phrase you get to use very often) to Fritz Lang's original *Dr Mabuse* film about a strange and sinister lunatic criminal with hypnotic powers. Mabuse uses his control to make opponents stand on useless hands and fold the nuts in poker.

6. *Silent Running* (1972)

The most surreal poker scene on film has got to be in Douglas Trumbull's first feature, co-written by Michael Cimino, the black comedy Sci Fi ecology film *Silent Running*. Having disposed of his fellow crew members, Bruce Dern flies off in a giant greenhouse and winds up playing poker with the robots that help look after its cargo of trees.

VARIETIES OF POKER

Jackpots

Jackpots, a variety of draw poker introduced in 1870, was an attempt to sober up the game by forbidding any player who held less than a pair of jacks or higher to open the betting.

THE SINGLE MOST IMPORTANT DECISION IN POKER

Choosing the right game is the most important choice you'll ever make as a player, writers Richard Harroch and Lou Krieger say: 'Choose the wrong game and little else matters. Choose the right game and you might even make money on a night when you're experiencing a below average run of cards.'

POKER ON PAPER

No one quite knows when faro was overtaken by poker as we now know it. Some time in the 1820s the new game appeared in New Orleans. For decades hundreds of regional variations were played across the United States. What we do know is that the first recorded game of what we'd recognise as poker happened in 1829. An English actor, Joseph Cowell, was travelling on one of the great Mississippi river boats, from Louisville to New Orleans. He saw a group of men playing cards and decided to take careful note of what they were doing.

Dramatically the boat ran aground during thick fog in the middle of the game, and while most of the passengers rushed to see what was going on one of the players, wearing green spectacles and a diamond stick pin, remained calmly shuffling the cards. Not calmly enough, however, it seems. Cowell recounts how, on their return, each player looked at their next hand, dealt by the man in the green spectacles, betting higher and higher as

they do so, unable to believe their luck. Round the table the players have increasingly good hands. What they don't know is the crooked dealer has given himself the best hand of all, a common trick among card sharps to encourage high betting. With four queens and an ace in hand, most poker players would, and did, bet the shirt off their back.

However, when the dealer looked at his cards he only had four 10s and an ace; in the confusion he's dealt himself the hand he intended for the first player, and given the young lawyer on his left 'his' winning hand. The lawyer happily pocketed over £2,000, leaving Cowell to sympathise with the con artist, and to reflect that a trip on a river boat is the perfect opportunity for 'the young merchant and their clerks to go at it with a perfect looseness, mixed up indiscriminately with vagabonds of all nations... All moral and social restraint was placed in the shade – there Jack was as good as his master.'

SOAP STARS OF POKER

There are clearly some good poker games going on behind the scenes of many of America's favourite shows. Celebrity poker tournaments have turned up whole tables of players in the case of *The West Wing*, and are dotted with entrants from series like *ER*, *The Practice* and *Law & Order*.

The West Wing
Martin Sheen • Mary McCormack
Allison Janney • Richard Schiff
John Spencer • Timothy Busfield

The Practice
Camryn Manheim • Steve Harris
Michael Badalucco

Law & Order
JK Simmons • Christopher Meloni

ER
Maura Tierney • Mekhi Phifer
Ming-Na

IT'S JUST MONOPOLY MONEY REALLY

Chip Reese, who broke in to the ranks of Vegas poker pros during the 1970s, is adamant that successful players cannot afford to think about the stakes when they're gambling. 'Money means nothing,' he says. 'If you really cared about it, you wouldn't be able to sit down at a poker table and bluff $50,000. It's just the yardstick by which you try to measure your success. In Monopoly, you try to win all the cash by the end of the game. It's the same in poker.'

Adds poet and literary critic Al Alvarez, a keen amateur: 'As it happens, Reese was speaking truer than he knew. I once played him in an impromptu game in London. The stakes were serious, but we had no chips, so the host filched his son's Monopoly set and we used the bills at their face value.'

You may be able to hide cards from your friends during the game, but rest assured you'll never be able to hide the fact that there was a game...

DOYLE BRUNSON'S GREATEST BLUFF

Poker wizard Doyle Brunson has pulled off many audacious bluffs during a stellar career, but none was greater than the one he attempted one evening in April 1988, miles from the nearest card table.

Brunson was returning home after winning a tournament, carrying $85,000 of uncashed casino chips in a pocket. As he reached his front door, he was surprised by two masked robbers who forced him into the house and bound both him and his wife together in their living room. The robbers made repeated threats to kill them unless they cooperated and handed over all the cash and jewellery they had.

Instead of complying, the 60-something Brunson bluffed, clutching his chest and feigning a massive heart attack. His attackers, fearing they could face a possible murder rap, panicked and ran. They left without so much as a dollar of the champion's money.

FOR WHEN ACTION BECOMES AN ADDICTION

Gamblers Anonymous, a self-help group for those 'willing to admit that gambling has them licked', first met in Los Angeles in September 1957. Since then the group has helped tens of thousands of compulsive gamblers to overcome their addiction.

GA, like Alcoholics Anonymous, bases its therapy on group meetings at which members tell their stories, discuss their problems and lend each other moral support. Like AA, Gamblers Anonymous has developed a 12-step programme for those who want to set out on the road to recovery. 'The programme,' they say, 'is fundamentally based on ancient spiritual principles and rooted in sound medical therapy. The best recommendation for the programme is the fact that "it works."' Here are the 12 steps which are a programme of recovery for the compulsive gambler:

1. We admitted we were powerless over gambling – that our lives had become unmanageable.
2. Came to believe that a Power greater than ourselves could restore us to a normal way of thinking and living.
3. Made a decision to turn our will and our lives over to the care of this Power of our own understanding.
4. Made a searching and fearless moral and financial inventory of ourselves.
5. Admitted to ourselves and to another human being the exact nature of our wrongs.
6. Were entirely ready to have these defects of character removed.
7. Humbly asked God (of our understanding) to remove our shortcomings.
8. Made a list of all persons we had harmed and became willing to make amends to them all.
9. Make direct amends to such people wherever possible, except when to do so would injure them or others.
10. Continued to take personal inventory and when we were wrong, promptly admitted it.
11. Sought through prayer and meditation to improve our conscious contact with God as we understood Him, praying only for knowledge of His will for us and the power to carry that out.
12. Having made an effort to practice these principles in all our affairs, we tried to carry this message to other compulsive gamblers.

You can contact Gamblers' Anonymous on 020 7384 3040. The group organises meetings throughout the UK, in Ireland and in 38 other countries, from Finland to Ethiopia. Friends and families of compulsive gamblers are invited to join Gamblers Anonymous, GA's sister organisation.

*Aces are larger than life and
greater than mountains.*

Mike Caro

POKER PUZZLERS

The answers. As if you needed them.

P10 A rounder is anyone who makes a living from playing poker professionally, so rounders are pros.

P20 River

P29 c) is the answer. As regards the other phrases...
a) A fish is a bad player, but seasoned players don't let them know how bad they are in order to encourage them to keep playing and losing. If one pro sees another being too obvious they'll say: 'Don't tap the aquarium', ie don't agitate the fish.
b) When you beat a big hand, like two aces hidden, you're said to have cracked the hand.
d) The muck is the pile of discarded cards before the dealer. When players send their cards back they are mucking their hands.
e) A rock is a slow and steady player, good, but predictable. Most other players would retreat if a 'rock' bet heavily at the end of a hand, but not if they have the 'nuts' – the best possible hand given what cards are already revealed on the table.

P36 b) 27%

P47 a) Seven-card stud high/low. All the others require you to use at least one card from those dealt to you.

P56 g) Patrick 'Ping-Pong' Klass. As regards the others folk...
a) Greg 'Fossilman' Raymer takes his nickname from the fossils he uses as card protectors at the table; b) 'Swami' Dennis Waterman – no relation to the *Minder* star – is a renowned US tournament player; c) as we went to press, the 'Prince of Docness', playing out of Santa Cruz, California, was ranked 772 in the world; d) Joe 'The Elegance' Beevers is a British member of the 'Hendon Mob', a group of players that emerged at the Poker Million tournament on the Isle of Man; e) 'Freeman' Dong, a tournament regular, makes his living as an actuary in Birmingham, Alabama; f) 'Madame Moustache' was a famed card cheat in the Old West hellhole of Bodie, California; h) 'Dream Crusher' Jenson is a renowned big-money cash-game player in the States.

P63 c)

P68 b) Barbara Enright finished fifth in 1995.

P78 b) Two pair, jacks and fives (Jackson 5).

P88 1E, 2C, 3H, 4B, 5F, 6G, 7D, 8A

P92 a) Run. Trips is a widely used term for three of a kind (from triple), in Texas hold 'em a set is when you're dealt a pair and a matching card comes up on the flop, and in seven-card stud you're rolled up if your first three cards are the same.

P105 d) 50%, because your opponent could also have the other two aces.

P112 A-Q. There are, Brunson is convinced, just too many ways of getting beaten with this apparently powerful hand. On the other hand, 'Texas Dolly' will almost always play the apparently much weaker 10-2. Those were the cards he held on both the occasions he won the World Series of Poker, in 1976 and 1977.

P117 b)

P125 b)

P137 a), c) and f)

P140 b)

Poker is a combination of luck and skill. People think mastering the skill part is hard, but they're wrong. The trick to poker is mastering the luck.

Jesse May

ACKNOWLEDGEMENTS

We gratefully acknowledge permission to reprint extracts of copyright material in this book from the following authors, publishers and executors:

Counsel to the President: A Memoir by Clark Clifford, copyright © 1991 by Clark Clifford. Used by permission of Random House, Inc.

Knights of the Green Cloth: The Saga of the Frontier Gamblers, by Robert K DeArment, published by University of Oklahoma Press, reproduced by permission of University of Oklahoma Press.

Big Deal, Anthony Holden, Copyright © Anthony Holden Ltd 1990. Reproduced by kind permission of Abacus, an imprint of Time Warner Book group Ltd.

Excerpt from *Positively Fifth Street, Murderers, Cheetahs and Binion's World Series of Poker* Copyright © 2003 by James McManus, reprinted by permission of Farrar Straus and Giroux LLC.
Positively Fifth Street by James McManus, Reprinted by permission of International Creative Management, Inc. Copyright © 2003 by James McManus.

Low Life: Lures and Snares of Old New York by Luc Sante, reprinted by kind permission of Grants Books.
Reprinted from *Low Life: Lures and Snares of Old New York* by Luc Sante. Copyright © 1991 by Luc Sante, reprinted by permission of The Joy Harris Agency, Inc.

The Championship Table at the World Series of Poker, by Smith, McEvoy and Wheeler, reproduced by permission of Cardoza Publishing.

INDEX

OTHER TITLES AVAILABLE IN THE SERIES

Poker Wit and Wisdom

By Fiona Jerome and Seth Dickson

From nineteenth-century Mississippi river boats to Cockney gambling dens and
.com casinos, *Poker Wit and Wisdom* takes a lingering look at the addictive world of
poker, dealing out all the oddities, quirks and stories along the way.

ISBN 1-84525-004-4

Wine Wit and Wisdom

By Maggie Rosen, Fiona Jerome and Seth Dickson

A lingering look at the wonderful world of wine, *Wine Wit and Wisdom* blends the
banquets of Bacchus with the grapes of wrath, and the fruitiest flavours with the
correct way to judge a bouquet.

ISBN 1-84525-003-6